A R C T I C
O C E A N

Greenland
(to Denmark)

Alaska
(part of US)

C A N A D A

Aleutian Islands *(part of US)*

St Pierre
and Miquelon
(to France)

P A C I F I C
O C E A N

UNITED STATES
OF AMERICA

Bermuda
(to UK)

A T L A N T I C
O C E A N

Midway Is.
(to US)

Wake Island
(to US)

Hawaii
(part of US)

Johnston Atoll
(to US)

MEXICO   BELIZE

MARSHALL
ISLANDS

Wallis
and Futuna
(to France)

Kingman Reef *(to US)*
Palmyra Atoll *(to US)*

GUATEMALA   HONDURAS
EL SALVADOR   NICARAGUA
COSTA RICA
PANAMA

Clipperton I.
(to French Polynesia)

VENEZUELA

Baker and Howland Is. *(to US)*
Jarvis I. *(to US)*

Galapagos Is.
(part of Ecuador)

COLOMBIA

French Guiana
(to France)

NAURU

K I R I B A T I

ECUADOR

GUYANA

SURINAME

TUVALU

Tokelau
(to NZ)

Cook Is.
(to NZ)

PERU

B R A Z I L

American
Samoa
(to US)

FIJI

Niue
(to NZ)

French Polynesia
(to France)

BOLIVIA

VANUATU
SOLOMON IS.

TONGA
SAMOA

Pitcairn Is.
(to UK)

PARAGUAY

Norfolk I.
(to Australia)

New
Caledonia
France)

NEW
ZEALAND

CHILE

URUGUAY

ARGENTINA

Chatham Is.
(part of NZ)

P A C I F I C
O C E A N

Bounty Is.
(part of NZ)

Campbell I.
(part of NZ)

South Georgia
and South
Sandwich Is.
(to UK)

Macquarie I.
(part of Australia)

Falkland Is.
(to UK)

SMITHSONIAN
HANDBOOKS

FLAGS

DK PUBLISHING

LONDON, NEW YORK, MUNICH,
MELBOURNE, DELHI

This book was produced in association with The Flag Institute, Chester, UK.

We would like to dedicate this book to the late Dr. William G. Crampton,
Director of the Flag Institute, without whom it would not have been possible.

Project Editor Siobhán Ryan
Project Designer David Douglas
Designers Tony Cutting, Carol Ann Davis, Yahya El Droubie,
Karen Gregory, Paul Williams
Editorial Contributors
Debra Clapson, Hayley Crockford, Michael Faul, Wim Jenkins,
Louise Keane, Nic Kynaston, Louisa Somerville
Managing Editor Lisa Thomas
Managing Art Editor Philip Lord
US Editor Mary Sutherland
DTP Systems Manager Tokiko Morishima
Production Controller David Proffit
Additional Illustrations Ciárán Hughes

First American Edition, 1997
4 6 8 10 9 7 5

Published in the United States by DK Publishing, Inc.
375 Hudson Street, New York, NY 10014

Copyright © 1997, 1998, 2001, 2002 Dorling Kindersley Limited, London
First published in 1997 as The Ultimate Pocket Flags of the World

Library of Congress Cataloging-in-Publication Data
Flags. -- 1st American ed.
      p. cm --(Eyewitness handbooks)
   Includes index.
   ISBN 0-7894-9084-6
   1. Flags--Handbooks, manuals, etc.   I. Series.
CR101.F398 1999.
929.9'2--dc21   98-38896
                                                                   CIP

Printed and bound in Hong Kong

see our complete product line at
www.dk.com

CONTENTS

NORTH & CENTRAL AMERICA

SOUTH AMERICA

AFRICA

EUROPE

ASIA

AUSTRALASIA & OCEANIA

INTRODUCTION

Flags are a part of everyday life. They are used by countries, provinces, cities, international bodies, organizations, and companies.

EARLY FLAGS

The earliest known flags were used in China, to indicate different parts of the army. In Europe flags began with the Roman *vexillum*, a square flag used by Roman cavalry, from which the term "vexillology" – the study of flags – originated. In the Middle Ages, heraldry became important as a means of identifying kings and lords. The distinctive coats of arms that developed were used as flags, and some still exist today.

FLAGS FOR IDENTIFICATION

The most significant development of flags was for use at sea. Ships flew flags for identification at a distance, and many of the rules of flag-use developed at sea. Some well-known flags were designed specifically for naval use, including the Dutch and Spanish flags *(see pages 123 & 138)* and the International code flags *(see page 238)*, which were used by ships to communicate with each other.

POLITICAL FLAGS

With the growth of independent nation states, flags have become more important in politics. Many newly independent states choose flags based on those of the political parties that secured independence. Revolutionary movements usually have their own flags, and private and professional organizations are increasingly adopting flags.

There are many different types of flags. This book deals with national, international, and subnational flags, and national coats of arms, arranged continent by continent. Among national flags are the state ensign and flag, for government use only on sea and land; the civil ensign and flag, for private and commercial use; and the naval ensign, flown by warships. Subnational flags may be of states (USA), provinces (Canada), cantons (Switzerland), overseas territories or other such areas.

KEY FLAGS IN WORLD HISTORY

Throughout history certain flags have become the inspiration of others, starting with the Stars and Stripes in 1777 *(see pages 13–14)*, which has inspired more flags than any other. The same degree of influence has been exercised by the French *Tricolore* from 1794, *(see page 133)*, the Dutch Tricolor *(see page 123)* and its major derivative the Russian Tricolor *(see page 168)*, which gave rise to most of the flags of eastern Europe. The next two pages summarize these key flags, whose "offspring" can be seen throughout this book.

KEY FLAGS IN WORLD HISTORY

THE DUTCH
(*PRINSENVLAG*)
FLAG, C. 1600

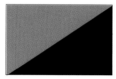

THE ANARCHIST
FLAG

The Dutch *Prinsenvlag* flag was adapted from the flags under which the Netherlands fought for independence from Spain in the 16th century. Orange was chosen to commemorate the leader, William of Orange, and blue and white were Christian colors. The *Prinsenvlag* was also the inspiration of the former flag of South Africa and of flags used in New York (formerly New Amsterdam).

This was first used during the French Revolution, as a variant of the Red Flag. The addition of black signified the idea of "Liberty or Death." In this form the flag was used in Haiti (1810), and influenced the German Tricolor of 1818. It was used throughout the 19th and 20th centuries as a political flag, and as such gave rise to the flags of Angola *(see page 96)* and is also used by the Sandinistas in Nicaragua.

THE BRITISH
RED ENSIGN

THE RED
FLAG

The idea for this flag emerged in the 17th century, and in Britain gave rise to the red ensign for civil use, the blue ensign for government or state use, and the white ensign for use on naval vessels. It is possible that the flag of the colonies in 1775 *(see page 13)*, which eventually led to the Stars and Stripes, was a variant of this flag. In the mid-19th century the blue ensign began to be used by colonial governments. After their independence, many colonies continued to use a red or blue ensign. In Rhodesia, Fiji, and Tuvalu, the field was changed to light blue.

The Red Flag dates back to the French Revolution. It was used again in the Paris Commune (1870) and in the Russian Revolution of 1905. Not until the success of the 1917 Bolshevik Revolution did it become the flag of Russia and later the Soviet Union (1924). It was copied by Communists in Vietnam, China, and Africa *(see pages 208 & 217)*. Even though many Communist regimes have now been supplanted, the Red Flag remains the flag of the extreme left and is widely used in one form or another as a left-wing party flag.

THE FLAG OF
FRANCISCO DE
MIRANDA, 1806

This was the first flag to symbolize emancipation from Spain in South America. A flag based on these colors was used for Colombia, Venezuela, and later Ecuador. The colors symbolized the blue ocean separating the South Americans (red) from the "tyrants" of Spain (yellow).

THE UNITED
PROVINCES OF
CENTRAL
AMERICA, 1823

This is the flag of the Central American provinces, which united to break away from Spain. It is not known whether the colors were derived from those of Argentina, or were indigenous to the region. Today, Nicaragua and El Salvador use flags closely resembling this one.

THE FLAG OF
MARCUS
GARVEY, 1806

Marcus Garvey was a black activist who sought a new home for black people in Africa. He imagined the flag of his "Ethiopia" to be black, red, and green. Garvey's movement was popular in the US in the 1920s and subsequently in Jamaica. The colors inspired many African politicians after World War II.

THE
RASTAFARIAN
FLAG

The coronation of Ras Tafari (Haile Selassie) as Emperor of Ethiopia in 1930 led to the formation of the Rastafarian movement in the West Indies. They adopted the flag of Ethiopia and added black from the Garvey flag, often in the form of a lion. The colors have since been used widely in Africa.

THE ARAB
REVOLT
FLAG,
1917

First used in the Hejaz, this flag quickly spread to Syria, Iraq, and Jordan. In 1920 the order of the stripes was changed to black-white-green. The red triangle symbolized the Hashemite rule and their descent from Muhammad. Today, King Hussein of Jordan is the only surviving ruler of this dynasty.

THE EGYPT
LIBERATION
MOVEMENT,
1953

This used the colors of the Arab Revolt flag and also introduced the eagle, said to have been the badge of Saladin. Originally it bore the then-Egyptian emblem on its breast. In 1956 it became the basis for the United Arab Republic flag and has been used since as the basis for many Arabic flags and arms.

TYPES OF FLAGS

 SALTIRE

A diagonal cross stretching from corner to corner of the flag.

 SCANDINAVIAN CROSS

A cross with the upright set closer to the hoist than to the fly.

 CROSS

A cross is vertical, centrally placed and extends across the whole flag.

 COUPED CROSS OR SALTIRE

A cross or saltire that ends short of the edges of the flag is couped.

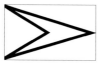 SERRATION

A flag where two colors are separated by a serrated edge.

 QUARTERED

A flag divided into four equal sections of differing design.

 FIMBRIATED

A narrow strip of color separating two broader stripes or larger areas.

 BICOLOR

A flag of two stripes of different colors, either horizontal or vertical.

TRICOLOR

A flag of three stripes of three colors, either horizontal or vertical.

 TRIANGLE

A flag divided by a triangle of a different color, usually at the hoist.

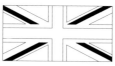 COUNTER-CHANGED

A charge placed on a line where two colors meet, which reverses them.

 BORDERED

A flag where the central color is surrounded by a different color.

PARTS OF THE FLAG

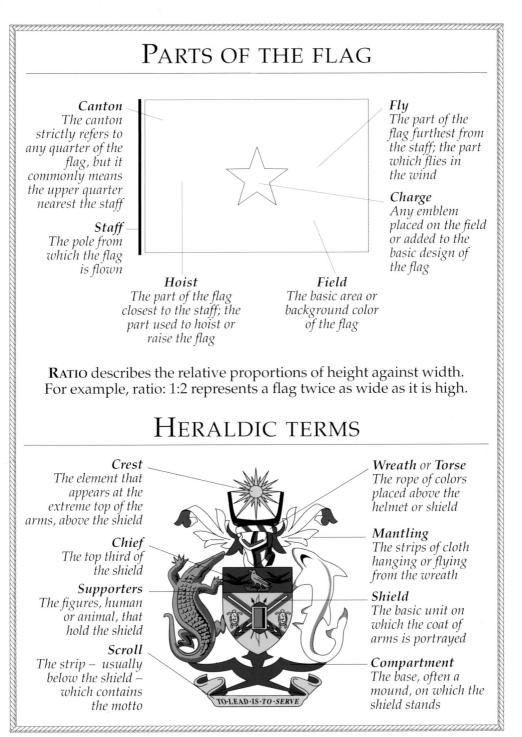

Canton
The canton strictly refers to any quarter of the flag, but it commonly means the upper quarter nearest the staff

Staff
The pole from which the flag is flown

Hoist
The part of the flag closest to the staff; the part used to hoist or raise the flag

Fly
The part of the flag furthest from the staff; the part which flies in the wind

Charge
Any emblem placed on the field or added to the basic design of the flag

Field
The basic area or background color of the flag

RATIO describes the relative proportions of height against width. For example, ratio: 1:2 represents a flag twice as wide as it is high.

HERALDIC TERMS

Crest
The element that appears at the extreme top of the arms, above the shield

Chief
The top third of the shield

Supporters
The figures, human or animal, that hold the shield

Scroll
The strip – usually below the shield – which contains the motto

Wreath or **Torse**
The rope of colors placed above the helmet or shield

Mantling
The strips of cloth hanging or flying from the wreath

Shield
The basic unit on which the coat of arms is portrayed

Compartment
The base, often a mound, on which the shield stands

TO·LEAD·IS·TO·SERVE

CANADA

Ratio: *1:2*   Adopted: *February 15, 1965*   Usage: *National and Civil*

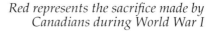

A stylized maple leaf has been Canada's national emblem for more than 150 years

White represents the snowy north of Canada

Red represents the sacrifice made by Canadians during World War I

NORTH AMERICA

CANADA BECAME A NATION in 1867 when four colonies united. Later, six other provinces and two territories joined the Confederation.

For many years Canada was without a national flag and used the British Red Ensign with the Canadian shield in the fly. In the early 1960s, pressure began to grow for a distinctive flag. The initial contender, known as "Pearson's Pennant," used maple leaves to represent Canada and a blue bar on either side representing the Pacific and Atlantic oceans.

THE NEW MAPLE LEAF FLAG
Pearson's Pennant did not meet with universal approval, and consensus was only reached on the idea of the maple leaf and on the use of the national colors. The result was the Maple Leaf Flag, which was adopted by Parliament in 1965. However, both the Union Jack and old red ensign remain in use.

CANADIAN RED ENSIGN

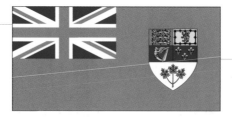

The Union Jack has been retained to symbolize Canada's link with the Commonwealth

The quarters of the shield represent England, France, Scotland, and Ireland – the homelands of many Canadian people

Canada – Provincial flags

THE DATE WHEN EACH province joined the Confederation is shown below the province name.

ALBERTA

1905

The shield dates from 1907 and was placed on a blue field to make a flag in 1967. The shield depicts a scene from the vast wheat lands of the west under St. George's Cross.

BRITISH COLUMBIA

1871

This flag, adopted in 1960, is an armorial banner of the coat of arms, granted in 1906. The sun placed over heraldic waters, represents the province's position on the west coast.

MANITOBA

1870

The flag is intended to recall and to preserve the old Canadian Red Ensign, with Manitoba's shield, depicting a buffalo on a rock, in the fly. It was adopted in 1966.

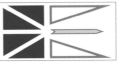

NEWFOUNDLAND & LABRADOR

1949

The colors of the flag attempt to represent all aspects of the province, such as snow, ice, and the sea. The design is intended to recall the Union Jack, the previous flag.

NEW BRUNSWICK

1867

Another armorial banner, authorized in 1965. The galley ship stands for shipbuilding, once an important industry, and the lion represents New Brunswick's ties to Britain.

NOVA SCOTIA

1867

Theoretically the oldest flag of a British Dominion. *Nova Scotia* means New Scotland. Its flag is a St. Andrew's Cross in reversed colors, with the Scottish Royal Arms.

ONTARIO

1867

The flag was adopted in 1965 and also attempts to recall and preserve the Canadian Red Ensign. The shield is from the arms of 1868 and was the first design to use a maple leaf.

PRINCE EDWARD ISLAND

1873

The flag is a banner of the coat of arms granted in 1905. It depicts an island, with a great British oak and its descendants, under the protection of a British lion.

 QUEBEC
1867

Adopted in 1948, this flag is a modern version of the *Fleurdelysé*, an old French-Canadian flag. The *fleur-de-lis* flower is symbolic of France.

 NORTHWEST TERRITORIES
1870

The flag was a competition winner in 1969. It contains the shield from the arms adopted in 1956. The lakes are represented by blue, snow by white.

 YUKON TERRITORY
1898

Accepted in 1967, the flag uses the 1956 coat of arms. Forests, snows and waters are symbolized by the colours.

 LABRADOR

The spruce sprigs on this regional flag denote the three races of the larger Newfoundland & Labrador Province.

 HM THE QUEEN OF CANADA

The Queen has often adopted royal standards for use in her various dominions, based on their own arms. The Canadian version dates from 1962.

 SASKATCHEWAN
1905

Adopted in 1969, the flag combines the provincial shield (representing forests and grain) with the floral emblem, the western red lily.

 NUNAVUT
1999

The figure on this flag symbolizes the stone monuments used to mark sacred places. The North Star represents the leadership of the community's elders.

 CAPE BRETON ISLAND

This competition-winning flag was adopted in 1994 by Cape Breton in Nova Scotia. The bird is a bald eagle.

GOVERNOR-GENERAL OF CANADA

This flag, dating from 1981, does not use the British Royal Crest; it has its own crest of a lion with a maple leaf.

United States of America

Ratio: *10:19*   Adopted: *1960*   Usage: *National and Civil*

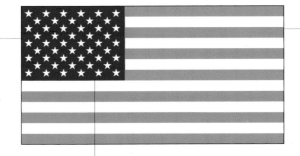

The 50 stars stand for each of the current states of the Union

13 stripes stand for the original 13 colonies that formed the United States

If a new state joins, a star is added the following July 4

North America

THE UNITED STATES was formed when 13 colonies rose against the British in 1775. They declared their independence from Britain on July 4, 1776.

The first flag used by the Americans was an adaptation of the British Red Ensign, known as the "Grand Union Flag," *(see page 14)*. From this developed the distinctive "Stars and Stripes," as it known today, that still has the 13 stripes for each of the original colonies to join the Union, and a star for each state that is now part of the US. The latest star was added on July 4, 1960, after Hawaii joined the US in 1959.

A TRULY NATIONAL FLAG

The flag of 1777 *(see page 14)*, marked a break with old colonial ties. It became the first of a new kind of flag, one that was truly a national flag in the modern sense. Its basic design and color combination was soon copied by other new nations.

The Stars and Stripes is an all-purpose flag, but the US is rich in flags of many other kinds.

THE PRESIDENT'S STANDARD

The Presidential Standard contains the President's version of the national coat of arms, and a ring of 50 stars. The insignia depicts an eagle holding a shield in the style of the Stars and Stripes, and 13 arrows and 13 olive leaves, indicating the country is prepared for either war or peace. The motto, *"E Pluribus Unum,"* meaning "Out of many, one," reflects the federal nature of the United States.

US – Historical flags

THE FLAGS OF THE Revolutionary War and the Civil War still have an influence on the American flags of today.

THE GRAND UNION FLAG

THE FIRST STARS AND STRIPES

The first American flag was adapted from the British Red Ensign of the time. It was known as the "Grand Union Flag," representing the Union of the 13 colonies. These were shown by the 13 stripes of red and white. It was introduced in December 1775 for use on land and at sea.

On June 14, 1777 the Union Jack was removed from the flag in favor of a blue canton with 13 stars, representing a new constellation, which now also represented the United States. This was the first use of stars in this way and set a precedent for many later flags.

THE FLAG OF 1795

THE FLAG OF 1818

When two new states joined the Union in 1795, two new stars and two new stripes were added to the flag, making 15 stripes and 15 stars. This set a precedent for adding new stripes and stars when each new state joined the Union. The flag soon became known as the "Star Spangled Banner."

Five new states were formed after 1795, but a new flag was not designed until 1817 when Congress decreed that only new stars would be added in the future, and it would revert to 13 stripes, to preserve the appearance of the flag. The new stars were added on July 4, 1818, and this system has been followed ever since.

THE STARS AND BARS

THE CONFEDERATE BATTLE FLAG

When the Southern states seceded from the Union in 1860, a new flag for the Confederacy was hoisted on March 4, 1861, known as the "Stars and Bars." It originally had 7 stars, but these increased to 13 in the course of 1861, as more states joined the Confederacy.

The Battle Flag with its distinctive saltire on a red field (southern cross) was introduced in September 1861, specifically for use in battle. On land it was square with a white border, but the rectangular naval version, without a border, is now accepted as the Confederate Flag.

US – State flags

THE DATE WHEN each state joined the Union is shown below the state name.

ALABAMA
1819

This flag, which was adopted in 1985, shows a red saltire on a white field. It is intended to recall the Southern Cross, or Battle Flag of the Confederate States.

ALASKA
1959

An Indian schoolboy designed the flag in 1926, when Alaska was still a territory. It depicts the Big Dipper and the northern Pole star. Gold also represents Alaska's mineral reserves.

ARIZONA
1912

The red and yellow rays recall the period of Spanish rule, and the copper star stands for mineral riches. The flag was designed locally and adopted in 1927.

ARKANSAS
1836

The lower stars represent former colonial powers that had controlled Arkansas and the upper star stands for the Confederacy. The flag was adopted in 1913.

CALIFORNIA
1850

The flag is based on that of the California Republic declared at Sonora in 1846; it did not become the state flag until 1911. It depicts a grizzly bear and a star for freedom.

COLORADO
1876

The C-shaped emblem contains the colors of Spain, which once laid claim to this area. The gold ball represents the state's mineral riches. The flag was adopted in 1911.

CONNECTICUT
1788

The coat of arms dates back to the seal of 1784, and the blue field to the Civil War period, when the flag was a Union color. This design was adopted in 1897.

DELAWARE
1787

The arms dates back to 1777, and the flag, adopted in 1913, includes the date Delaware joined the Union. The colors recall the uniforms worn during the Revolutionary War.

DISTRICT OF
COLUMBIA

1791

The flag of the Federal District of
Columbia is based on a banner of the
arms of the Washington family,
which originated in England and
dates back to 1592. It was adopted in
1938 by a Congress Commission.

FLORIDA

1845

This is another flag that recalls the
southern cross used by the
Confederacy during the Civil War.
The original flag, adopted in 1868,
had only the seal, the red saltire was
added in 1900.

GEORGIA

1788

The new state flag for Georgia
was introduced in 2001, following
objections to the previous design's
emphasis on the Confederate flag.
The yellow ribbon contains former
flags of Georgia and the US.

HAWAII

1959

The state flag, originally
representing the independent
kingdom, was adopted in 1845. The
Union Jack recalls a flag given to the
king by an army officer in 1793. The
stripes stand for the main islands.

IDAHO

1890

The flag was originally a military
color and bears the state seal in the
center; beneath it is a scroll with the
state's name. The flag in this form
was adopted in 1927, with new
specifications in 1957.

ILLINOIS

1818

Created in 1915, the central emblem
of the Illinois flag depicts elements
from the state seal, including a bald
eagle and a shield of the Stars and
Stripes. The name was added
beneath this in 1970.

INDIANA

1816

The flag was the winning entry in a
design competition held in 1916 and
was officially adopted in 1917. The
stars in two arcs are for the original
states and the subsequent ones.

IOWA

1846

The red, white, and blue colors stand
for French Louisiana, of which Iowa
was once a part. In the center is the
seal of 1847. The flag was adopted in
this form in 1921.

KANSAS

1861

The flag of Kansas follows a very common seal and name pattern. The original flag of 1925 had the seal, recalling settlement and agriculture, and a sunflower – the state flower. The name was added in 1963.

KENTUCKY

1792

Another flag derived from the militia colors. The flag was adopted in 1918 and regularized in 1962. Like many state flags it contains the seal, the state name, and a wreath of the state flower, in this case, golden rod.

LOUISIANA

1812

The pelican, representing self-sacrifice and the state's role as a protector, has long been the badge of Louisiana, but the flag was finally adopted in 1912. The Acadians have their own flag.

MAINE

1820

The flag dates from 1909 when the arms, adopted in 1820, were placed on a blue field. The star and motto recall Maine's northerly location. It was the northernmost state of the Union, until Michigan joined in 1837.

MARYLAND

1788

This is the only state flag that is a true heraldic banner, reproducing the arms of the Baltimore family, once the proprietors of the state. Each side of the family is represented by two quarters. It was adopted in 1904.

MASSACHUSETTS

1788

The flag was originally adopted in 1908 and revised in 1971, replacing a pine tree with the coat of arms adopted in 1780. The arms, depicting an Indian holding a bow, now appears on both sides of the flag.

MICHIGAN

1837

The arms, adopted in 1832, was placed on a blue field to make the state flag in 1911. The mottoes mean "I will defend," and "If you seek a pleasant peninsula, look about you."

MINNESOTA

1858

The motto on this flag "The North Star," was retained from when the state was the most northerly in the Union. The flag was originally adopted in 1893 and revised in 1957.

MISSISSIPPI

1817

The flag of Mississippi was adopted in 1894. It combines both the Confederacy's southern cross with the stripes of its first flag, the Stars and Bars, although on the flag of Mississippi the upper stripe is blue.

 MISSOURI

1821

The colors of the flag recall when the region was under French control. The 24 stars stand for Missouri as the 24th state to join the Union. Within the seal itself are another 24 stars. The flag was adopted in 1913.

 MONTANA

1889

The flag is derived from the former state militia colors, while the motto, "Gold and Silver" is in Spanish, recalling Spain's claim to the area. The flag was adopted in 1905 and the name was added in 1981.

 NEBRASKA

1867

The flag of Nebraska was adopted in 1925 and uses the seal that was adopted in 1867. This depicts an allegorical landscape, symbolic of the state's agricultural and industrial development.

 NEVADA

1864

The flag emerged from a design competition and was adopted in 1929. It was revised in 1991 and the state name was placed underneath boughs of the sage bush, and the star that represents the state.

 NEW HAMPSHIRE

1788

The design was adopted in 1909, making use of the seal, which dates back to 1775. It depicts a ship, the *Raleigh*, being built on the stocks at the town of Portsmouth during the Revolutionary War.

 NEW JERSEY

1787

The buff field recalls the uniforms worn during the Revolutionary War. The flag with the coat of arms was adopted in 1896 and made generally available in 1938.

 NEW MEXICO

1912

This most distinctive flag was adopted in 1925 and uses the sun symbol of the *Zia Pueblo* Indians, while the colors represent the Spanish colonial era.

NEW YORK

1788

The flag dates originally from flags used in the Revolutionary War, but in this form only from 1901. Prior to that the flag had a buff field. The two figures symbolize liberty and justice. The coat of arms dates from 1777.

NORTH CAROLINA

1789

The original flag was adopted in 1861 at the outbreak of the Civil War and used the same colors as the Stars and Bars. The present design dates from 1885. It contains the initials of the state in the blue stripe.

NORTH DAKOTA

1889

The flag was originally used by the state militia, the North Dakota Infantry, and was adopted in 1911, almost without alteration, explaining its squarish shape. In the center is a version of the national arms.

OHIO

1803

The pennant-shaped flag of Ohio is derived from a cavalry guidon of the Civil War period. The 17 stars represent Ohio as the 17th state to join the union and the circle, or "O" refers to the state's initial.

OKLAHOMA

1907

The basic design emerged from a competition and was adopted in 1925. The name Oklahoma was added in 1941. The Indian peace emblems recall the previous designation of Indian Territory.

OREGON

1859

This is now the only state flag with a different design on its reverse. The obverse shows the seal within 33 stars, the state's name, and its date of admission. The reverse shows a beaver. It was adopted in 1925.

PENNSYLVANIA

1787

The coat of arms of the state was adopted in 1777 and regularized in 1875. It was placed on a blue field to make the flag in 1907. The shield is supported by two horses.

RHODE ISLAND

1790

The anchor, symbolic of hope, has long been the emblem of Rhode Island. The flag, based on a Revolutionary War flag, was adopted in 1877 and modified in 1897.

SOUTH CAROLINA
1788

The flag was adopted in 1861 at the very start of the Civil War, but contains emblems used during the Revolutionary War and also used in the state arms. The palmetto in the center is the state tree.

SOUTH DAKOTA
1889

The flag of South Dakota was adopted in 1963 on the basis of previous models and had the former motto "The Sunshine State" around the seal. This was changed to "The Mount Rushmore State" in 1992.

TENNESSEE
1796

The three stars indicate that the state was the third to join the Union after the original 13 states, and its general appearance recalls the Confederate Battle Flag or southern cross. The flag was adopted in 1905.

TEXAS
1845

The flag copies the colors of the Stars and Stripes but has only one star, which dates back to the one on the plain blue flag of the Republic of Texas. It was adopted in 1839 and retained after Texas joined the Union.

UTAH
1896

The beehive in the flag recalls the emblem of the Mormon state of Deseret, located in Utah, and the date recalls their settlement of the region. The present flag dates from 1911, and uses the seal adopted in 1896.

VERMONT
1791

The arms, including the Lone Pine emblem, date back to when Vermont was independent from 1777–91. The present flag, based on the former militia flag, was adopted in 1923. The state name appears on a scroll.

VIRGINIA
1788

The state arms was adopted in 1776. The seal, showing a victorious warrior, was placed on the flag in 1861 at the start of the Civil War. The design has been used ever since.

WASHINGTON
1889

Washington is known as "The Evergreen State" and this is reflected by its flag. It is the only state with a green flag. The seal dates from 1889 and was placed on the flag in 1923.

WEST VIRGINIA

1863

The coat of arms dates from 1863 when West Virginia seceded from Virginia. The current version of the flag was adopted in 1929 and has the arms within a wreath of rhododendron, the state flower.

WISCONSIN

1848

The flag is derived from the militia colors of the Union in 1863. It depicts the state seal, supported by a miner and a sailor. The shield also recalls mining and sailing. The name and the date were added in 1980.

WYOMING

1890

The flag emerged from a design competition and was adopted in 1917. The flag has been revised several times, at one time the buffalo containing the arms faced the fly. The colors recall the national flag.

AMERICAN SAMOA

A self-governing US dependency, American Samoa's flag contains many associations with its protectorate, not only in the colors of the flag but also the emblem, which is an American bald eagle.

GUAM

The flag was designed locally and adopted in 1917. In the center of the flag, in the US colors, is the seal of the territory, which depicts an idealized landscape. The flag can be flown only with the US flag.

NORTHERN MARIANA ISLANDS

The original flag was adopted in 1972 but has undergone several modifications, including the addition of the flower wreath. It also depicts a gray *latte* stone representing the islands' *Chamorro* culture.

PUERTO RICO

The resemblance of this flag to that of Cuba is no coincidence, since the two were designed at the same time. This version was adopted in 1952 and may be flown only with the US flag.

VIRGIN ISLANDS (US)

The flag dates from 1921 and uses part of the US seal, with the initials of the islands. The three arrows in one claw stand for the main islands; in the other claw is an olive branch.

MEXICO

Ratio: 4:7   Adopted: *November 2, 1821*   Usage: *National and Civil*

The basic design is derived from the French Tricolore

Red, white, and green are the colors of the national liberation army in Mexico

The coat of arms incorporates the badge of Mexico City

MEXICO WAS CONQUERED by Spain in the 16th century but broke away in 1821 to form a Central American state. It became a republic in 1822.

France was the inspiration of those who detached Mexico from Spain in 1821, and they devised a new tricolor based on the flag of the liberation army. At that time the Italian tricolor was not in use.

The flag now contains the coat of arms, in order to distinguish it from that of Italy.

THE AZTEC INHERITANCE
The central emblem is the Aztec pictogram for Tenochtitlán (now Mexico City), the center of their empire. It recalls the legend that inspired the Aztecs to settle on what was originally a lake-island.

The form of the coat of arms was most recently revised in 1968.

ARMS OF MEXICO

The lake with an island represents Tenochtitlán

Aztec legend held that they should found their city on the spot where they saw an eagle on a cactus, eating a snake

Ribbon in the national colors

GUATEMALA

Ratio: *5:8*   Adopted: *August 17, 1871*   Usage: *National and State*

Blue and white
are the colors of
the original flag
of the United
Provinces of
Central America

The Guatemalan
coat of arms
was adopted
in 1968

NORTH
AMERICA

GUATEMALA DECLARED independence at the same
time as Mexico and, in 1823, became part of a
union with the other Central American states.

In Guatemala, the Central American flag *(see page 7)* was used until 1851 when a pro-Spanish faction took over and added the Spanish colors of red and yellow to the flag. On August 17, 1871 the original colors were restored, but in vertical, rather than horizontal stripes and with a new coat of arms.

THE QUETZAL BIRD

The new coat of arms shows the quetzal, Guatemala's most famous bird, standing on a scroll that gives the date of Guatemala's Declaration of Independence. The present form of the arms was adopted in 1968.

When used at sea for civil purposes, the flag does not contain the arms.

ARMS OF GUATEMALA

The date of its
Declaration of
Independence

Rifles and swords
represent defense
of freedom

The quetzal bird
with its
distinctive tail-
feathers is a
symbol of liberty

BELIZE

Ratio: 3:5   Adopted: September 21, 1981   Usage: National and Civil

The coat of arms was granted in 1907

Blue is the party color of the PUP

The 50 leaves recall 1950, the year the PUP came to power

Red stripes were added to denote the color of the opposition party

Mexico   BELIZE
Guatemala

BELIZE WAS originally known as British Honduras, a colony formed in 1862 from settlements on the coast of Guatemala.

British Honduras obtained a coat of arms on January 28, 1907, which formed the basis of the badge used on British ensigns. The coat of arms recalls the logging industry that first led to British settlement there.

From 1968 onward an unofficial national flag was in use. It was blue, with a modified version of the arms – minus the Union Jack – on a white disk in the center. The colors were those of the People's United Party (PUP). Around the arms was a wreath of 50 leaves, remembering 1950, when the PUP came to prominence.

On independence in 1981, the flag was retained, but red was added to stand for the opposition party.

ARMS OF BELIZE

The figures, tools, and the mahogany tree represent the logging industry

Wreath of 50 leaves

National motto – Sub Umbra Floreo *meaning* "I Flourish in the Shade"

EL SALVADOR

Ratio: *1:2*   Adopted: *May 17, 1912*   Usage: *National and State*

The flag is modeled on the flag of the United Provinces of Central America

The emblem is surrounded by the national flags of the members of the United Provinces of Central America

The title of the state while it was part of the United Provinces of Central America surrounds the emblem

NORTH AMERICA

Guatemala   Honduras
EL SALVADOR

EL SALVADOR'S FLAG recalls the colors of the United Provinces of Central America, used following independence from Spain in 1823.

The flag of Central America (*see page 7*) was used as the national flag until 1865, when a flag based on the Stars and Stripes was adopted, with blue and white stripes and a red canton containing nine stars.

In 1912 the original design was readopted, with the arms of El Salvador in the center.

TRIANGLES AND VOLCANOES

The coat of arms is similar to those of the United Provinces of Central America. The emblem is based on the Masonic triangle representing equality and depicts the five original provinces with five volcanoes. Around the triangle are five national flags and a wreath, tied in the national colors.

ARMS OF EL SALVADOR

A triangle representing equality

The motto of Central America – Dios, Union, Libertad *meaning* "God, Union, Liberty"

The Cap of Liberty

Five volcanoes representing the original united provinces

HONDURAS

Ratio: *1:2*   Adopted: *February 16, 1866*   Usage: *National and Civil*

The colors and pattern are the same as the flag of the United Provinces of Central America

Five stars represent the five original members of the United Provinces of Central America

NORTH AMERICA

HONDURAS WAS ONE of the Spanish colonies that formed the United Provinces of Central America in 1823. It became independent in 1838.

In 1823 Honduras joined the United Provinces of Central America and adopted their flag *(see page 7)*. In 1866 it was amended; five blue stars were placed in the center to represent the five original Central American provinces. The state flag has the coat of arms of Honduras in the center in place of the stars.

The coat of arms was created in 1838 and revised in 1935. At the center is a Maya pyramid rising from the sea. Around this is a band with the name of the state and the date of its Declaration of Independence. Beneath it is a landscape with allegorical items representing mineral and timber industries.

ARMS OF HONDURAS

The cornucopias are symbolic of prosperity and agricultural wealth

A Maya pyramid

The landscape depicts mines, mining tools, forests, and logging tools

NICARAGUA

Ratio: *3:5*   Adopted: *September 4, 1908*   Usage: *National and Civil*

Apart from the text around the arms, the flag is identical to that of the United Provinces of Central America

The coat of arms of Nicaragua

"America Central" recalls the United Provinces of Central America

NORTH AMERICA

NICARAGUA DECLARED independence from Spain in 1821. It was a member of the United Provinces of Central America from 1823 to 1838.

The flag and the arms of Nicaragua in use today are the most similar to those used by the United Provinces of Central America. The triangle, volcanoes, rising sun, Cap of Liberty, and rainbow all appeared on the original emblem. The coat of arms used today contains the name of the state, *Republica de Nicaragua*, whereas in 1823 the title was *Provincias Unidas del Centro de America.*

The decision to revert to the emblems used by the United Provinces of Central America was taken in 1908 and reflected Nicaragua's aspirations for the rebirth of the political entity formed by the five nations.

ARMS OF NICARAGUA

The five volcanoes represent the original five member states

The rays of the sun and the rainbow are symbolic of the bright future

The Cap of Liberty represents national freedom

COSTA RICA

Ratio: *3:5*   Adopted: *September 29, 1848*   Usage: *National and State*

Blue and white were the colors of the original flag of the United Provinces of Central America

Red, white, and blue recall the colors of the French Tricolore

NORTH
AMERICA

COSTA RICA WAS a signatory to the Declaration of Independence from Spain in 1821, joining the United Provinces of Central America (1823–1838).

The Central American flag remained in use in Costa Rica until 1848 when, in response to events in France, it was decided to incorporate the French colors into the national flag. This was done by adding a central red stripe. The coat of arms was also revised and placed in the center of the flag. In 1906, it was placed in a white disk on the red stripe, and later on an oval, set toward the hoist.

The coat of arms depicts the isthmus between the Pacific Ocean and the Caribbean Sea. The stars stand for the seven provinces, and the Central American union is recalled by *America Central* on the upper scroll.

ARMS OF COSTA RICA

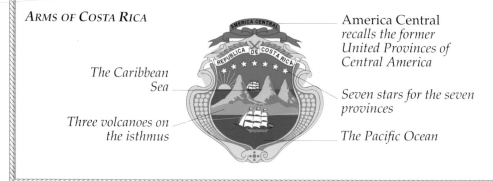

America Central recalls the former United Provinces of Central America

Seven stars for the seven provinces

The Pacific Ocean

The Caribbean Sea

Three volcanoes on the isthmus

28

PANAMA

Ratio: 2:3 Adopted: *November 3, 1903* Usage: *National and Civil*

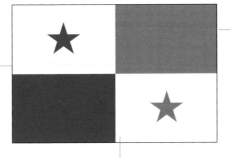

Although inspired by the Stars and Stripes, the stars and quarters are said to represent the two main political parties

Red was the color of the Conservatives and blue that of the Liberals

White symbolizes peace in the country

PANAMA, ORIGINALLY a province of Colombia, was detached in 1903 to secure the building of the Panama Canal within a US-controlled zone.

The first flag, proposed in 1903, consisted of seven horizontal stripes of red and yellow, with a blue canton containing two golden suns, joined by a narrow line to depict the oceans to be united by the Panama Canal.

However this was not accepted by the Panamanian leader, Manuel A. Guerrero, whose family designed a new flag. Although clearly modeled on the flag of the US, the stars and quarters are said to stand for the rival political parties, and the white for the peace in which they operate.

The coat of arms reflects Panama's transition from civil war to peace, and the increased prosperity this promised the people.

ARMS OF PANAMA

The shield depicts tools, weapons, a cornucopia and a winged wheel, which together symbolize a move from war to peace and prosperity

The national motto – Pro Mundi Benefico meaning "For the benefit of the World"

The Northern and Southern Hemispheres joined by the Panama Canal

JAMAICA

Ratio: *1:2*   Adopted: *August 6, 1962*   Usage: *National and Civil*

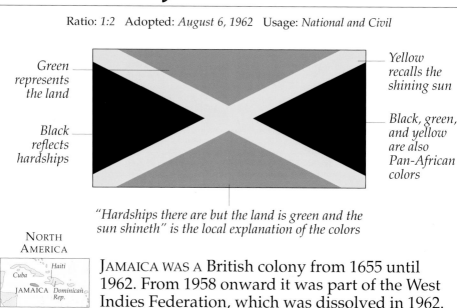

Green represents the land

Black reflects hardships

Yellow recalls the shining sun

Black, green, and yellow are also Pan-African colors

"Hardships there are but the land is green and the sun shineth" is the local explanation of the colors

NORTH AMERICA

JAMAICA WAS A British colony from 1655 until 1962. From 1958 onward it was part of the West Indies Federation, which was dissolved in 1962.

The present design emerged from those sent in by the public in a national competition. It was originally designed with vertical stripes, but this was considered too similar to the Tanganyikan flag, and so the saltire was substituted.

The coat of arms, based on that granted to Jamaica on February 3, 1663, is among the oldest granted to a British colony. It was used on the former British flags of Jamaica.

THE QUEEN'S STANDARD
The flag for HM Queen Elizabeth II was introduced after independence. It contains a banner of the arms, with the Queen's Cypher in the center. The shield depicts the red Cross of St. George charged with pineapples.

BANNER OF THE QUEEN OF JAMAICA

The Royal Cypher is enclosed within a chaplet of roses

St. George's Cross

The four pineapples and cross are taken from the coat of arms of Jamaica

CUBA

Ratio: *1:2*   Adopted: *May 20, 1902*   Usage: *National and Civil*

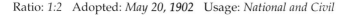

La
Estrella
Solitaria
– *the Lone
Star*

*The
design is
based on
the US
Stars and
Stripes*

*The triangle comes from the Masonic
symbol for equality*

NORTH
AMERICA

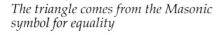

CUBA, **the only Communist state in the Americas,
was a Spanish colony until 1898, when it was
ceded to the US. It gained independence in 1902.**

The flag was designed in 1848 for the
liberation movement, which sought
to detach Cuba from Spain and make
it into a state of the US. The Lone
Star represented another star that
would be added to "the splendid
North American constellation."
The triangle is derived from the
Masonic symbol for equality, while
the five stripes stand for the five
provinces of the time. The flag was
briefly hoisted in 1850 at Cardenas
but was not officially adopted until
1902, when independence was
granted by the US.

Another flag from the 19th century
is that of Carlos Manuel de
Céspedes, used by the independence
movement of 1868–78. It is now used
as the flag of the Cuban navy.

FLAG OF CÉSPEDES

*The flag is like that of
Chile with the blue
and red reversed*

*This flag was also
modeled on the Stars
and Stripes, using the
same colors: blue, red,
and white and a star in
the canton*

BAHAMAS

Ratio: *1:2* Adopted: *July 10, 1973* Usage: *National*

Black
represents
the strength
of the people

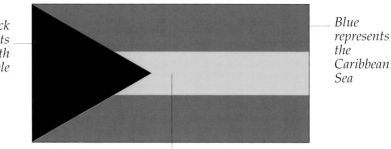

Blue
represents
the
Caribbean
Sea

Yellow reflects the islands' sandy beaches

NORTH
AMERICA

ORIGINALLY A PIRATE BASE, the Bahamas became a formal British colony in 1783. It did not achieve independence until July 10,1973.

The colors of the flag are intended to represent the aquamarine water around the islands and their golden sands. The flag is based on designs by the Bahamian people. Many of those submitted also included the idea of sunrise, which has been incorporated into the coat of arms.

The Bahamas Civil Ensign (flown by merchant ships) is often seen, since many ships are registered in the Bahamas. The flag is based on the British Red Ensign – red with a Bahamian national flag in the canton – but is distinguished by the white cross, like the Cross of St. George, across the red field.

The Bahamas has many other flags, including one for the specific use of the Prime Minister.

BAHAMAS CIVIL ENSIGN

The national flag is placed in the canton

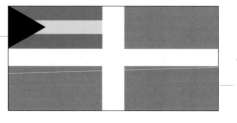

The civil ensign is distinguished from government and naval ensigns by its red field

HAITI

Ratio: *3:5*   Adopted: *May 18, 1803*   Usage: *National and Civil*

*For official and
state purposes
the flag is
charged with the
national arms
on a central
white disk*

Blue and
red are
taken
from the
French
Tricolore

NORTH
AMERICA

HAITI BECAME A French colony in 1697, but in 1803 a rebellion broke out. Independence was granted on January 1, 1804.

The blue and red of the flag were retained after a French *Tricolore* was torn up by the rebel Jean-Jacques Dessalines in 1803. The two parts were stitched together horizontally to make a new flag.

However, a rival flag of vertical black and red panels was also used at various times, most recently in the period from 1964–86, during the regime of the Duvalier family.

Since 1843 the flag for official and state use has had the arms on a white panel in the center. The coat of arms depicts a trophy of weapons ready to defend freedom and a royal palm topped with a Cap of Liberty for the country's independence.

ARMS OF HAITI

The Cap of Liberty

*The royal palm
symbolizes
independence*

*Weapons reflect the
people's willingness
to defend their liberty*

The national motto –
L'Union Fait La
Force *meaning
"Union is Strength"*

L'UNION FAIT LA FORCE

DOMINICAN REPUBLIC

Ratio: *2:3*   Adopted: *November 6, 1844*   Usage: *National and State*

Blue and red are taken from the flag of Haiti, which once controlled the Dominican Republic

The coat of arms only appears on the flag for national and state use

The cross of the Trinitarian independence movement

NORTH AMERICA

A SPANISH COLONY, briefly occupied by Haiti (1820–44), the Trinitarian movement was formed to free the country. It was liberated in 1844.

The flag was designed by the leader of the Trinitarians. He altered the layout of the blue and red of the Haitian flag, placing a large white cross over it to symbolize faith.

A DISTINCTIVE NATIONAL FLAG
To create distinct flags for state and civil use, the coat of arms, adopted in 1844, was placed on the state flag. The civil flag, on both land and sea, does not carry the coat of arms.

The arms depicts a Bible open at the first chapter of St. John's Gospel. This is placed on a trophy of national flags, on a shield of the same design. The Trinitarian motto is above this and the name of the state below.

ARMS OF THE DOMINICAN REPUBLIC

Gospel of St. John, a Trinitarian emblem

The password of the Trinitarian movement – Dios, Patria, Libertad ("God, Country, Freedom")

The lower scroll contains the state title

ST. KITTS & NEVIS

Ratio: 2:3   Adopted: *September 19, 1983*   Usage: *National and Civil*

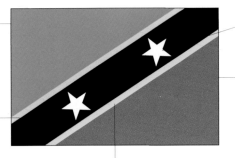

Green is symbolic
of the fertile land

Two stars for hope
and liberty

Black recalls
St. Kitts's
African heritage

Red recalls the
struggle for
freedom

Yellow reflects the country's
sunny climate

NORTH
AMERICA

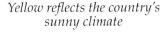

A BRITISH COLONY in the Leeward Islands since 1873, the islands of St. Kitts and Nevis gained independence together in 1983.

The flag was the winning entry in a local competition that attracted 258 entries and was the work of a student, Edrice Lewis. It was she who gave what is now the official interpretation of the flag – that its colors stand for the fertile land, year-round sunshine, the struggle for freedom and the African heritage. The two stars stand for hope and

liberty, not for the islands of St. Kitts and Nevis.

THE FLAG OF NEVIS

The island of Nevis has a flag of its own, which is bright yellow with a stylized image of Nevis Peak. The national flag is in the canton.

St. Kitts also has an ensign for the Coast Guard.

THE FLAG OF NEVIS

National flag
in canton

A graphic
representation of
Nevis Peak, a
cone-shaped
mountain in the
center of the island

Yellow for
year-long
sunshine

ANTIGUA & BARBUDA

Ratio: 2:3   Adopted: *February 27, 1967*   Usage: *National and Civil*

Black recalls the
islands' African
heritage

The rising sun
represents a
new era

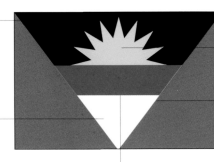

White
symbolizes hope

The V-shape is the
symbol of victory

Blue represents the Caribbean Sea

NORTH
AMERICA

FROM 1632 UNTIL formal independence was
granted in 1981, Antigua and its neighbor
Barbuda were British colonies.

The flag dates from the achievement
of self-government in 1967. It was the
winning design in a competition that
more than 600 local people entered.

THE SYMBOLISM OF THE FLAG
The designer Reginald Samuel
interpreted it as representing the sun
rising against the background of the
peoples' African heritage in a new
era. The overall V-shape stands for
victory. It is on a red background
that symbolizes the dynamism of the
population. Blue is for the sea, and
white is for hope.

THE NEW NATIONAL FLAG
The flag was retained unchanged
when Antigua became independent.

Barbuda does not have a separate
flag, although there is one for
Redonda, an uninhabited island
whose "throne" is claimed by several
rival "monarchs."

THE NATIONAL ARMS
The coat of arms was granted in 1977
and depicts a shield with a sugar
mill, once the primary industry, on a
background of white and blue
waves. Above this is a sun on a black
background. The shield stands on a
sea island. The crest is a pineapple
from the arms of the former colony
of the Leeward Islands, of which
Antigua was once a part. Beneath is
a scroll with the national motto –
"Each endeavouring, all achieving."

DOMINICA

Ratio: *1:2*   Adopted: *November 3, 1978*   Usage: *National and Civil*

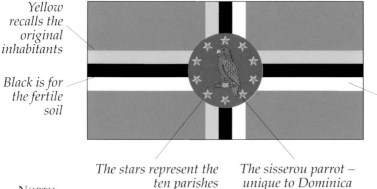

Yellow recalls the original inhabitants

Black is for the fertile soil

White symbolizes the region's pure water

The stars represent the ten parishes

The sisserou parrot – unique to Dominica

NORTH AMERICA

Puerto Rico   Guadeloupe
DOMINICA
Martinique

FIRST COLONIZED by the French, Dominica came under British control in 1759. It became a British Associated State in 1967 and independent in 1978.

The flag, adopted in 1978, features the national bird emblem, the sisserou parrot, which also appears on the coat of arms granted July 21, 1961. This parrot is unique to Dominica. It is an endangered species; only a few pairs remain.

The green field represents the lush vegetation of the island. The cross represents the Trinity and the Christian faith, and its three colors recall the native Indians, the fertile soil, and the pure water. The ten stars stand for the ten parishes and the red disk for social justice.

The flag of the President has a dark green field with the coat of arms in the center, crowned with a British lion. It depicts palm trees, an indigenous frog, and the sea.

THE PRESIDENT'S FLAG

The supporters are two sisserou parrots

The national motto is in Creole – Aprés Bondie C'est La Ter meaning "After the good Lord (we love) the soil"

ST. LUCIA

Ratio: *1:2*   Adopted: *March 1, 1967*   Usage: *National and Civil*

The blue field represents the sea

This symbol represents twin peaks of the Pitons – two famous volcanic mountains

NORTH AMERICA

Dominica
Martinique
ST. LUCIA
St. Vincent &
The Grenadines
Barbados

ST. LUCIA, first settled in 1605, was fought over by the French and the British, finally ceding to Britain in 1814. It became independent in 1979.

The flag was adopted when St. Lucia became a British Associated State in 1967. It was designed by a local artist, Dunstan St. Omer. The blue field represents the sea, from which the peaks of the Pitons are said to be "rising sheer out of the sea and looking skyward – a symbol of hope." The yellow triangle stands for sunshine and the black arrowhead on white for the twin cultures of the island. On independence, the flag was retained, but the height of the yellow triangle was increased.

A new form of the coat of arms symbolized the national motto: "The Land, the People, the Light." Apart from the Governor-General's flag and that of the capital, Castries, no other flags are known.

THE GOVERNOR-GENERAL'S STANDARD

The Royal Crest of England, with a British lion and crown

The state's title is placed on the scroll

SAINT LUCIA

St. Vincent & the Grenadines

Ratio: 2:3   Adopted: *October 12, 1985*   Usage: *National and Civil*

Blue recalls the sky

Yellow represents sunshine

Green represents the islands' abundant vegetation

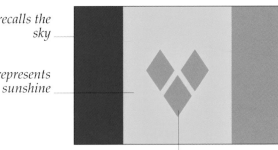

The "Gems of the Antilles"

North America

ST. VINCENT WAS OCCUPIED by the British in 1762. It achieved independence in 1979, together with the Grenadines, a chain of adjacent islands.

The basic design and colors of the flag date from the flag hoisted on the day of independence in 1979. It had the coat of arms of the islands placed on a stylized breadfruit leaf in the center. Its blue, yellow, and green stripes were derived from the common colors of the flags assigned to the Associated States by the College of Arms. The breadfruit recalled the British introduction of the breadfruit tree into the Caribbean from the South Seas. Although this first flag was designed by a local islander, the design did not please all the people of St. Vincent and the Grenadines, and, in 1985, moves were made to secure a new design.

A NEW NATIONAL FLAG
After a local competition failed to produce a satisfactory design, the problem was submitted to a Swiss graphic artist who suggested what is now the current design. In this, the "V" formed by the diamonds stands for St. Vincent, and the diamonds represent the local sobriquet as the "Gems of the Antilles."

THE COAT OF ARMS OF ST. VINCENT
The coat of arms was first introduced in 1912. It depicts two women, one standing holding an olive branch, the other kneeling to represent peace and justice, which is the national motto – *Pax, Justitia*. This appears on a scroll at the base.

BARBADOS

Ratio: *2:3*   Adopted: *November 30, 1966*   Usage: *National and Civil*

Blue represents the sea

The broken trident represents a break with the past

Gold reflects the golden sands of Barbados

NORTH AMERICA

St. Vincent & The Grenadines   BARBADOS

Grenada

BARBADOS WAS FIRST settled by the British in 1627. It became a colony and achieved self-government in 1961 and independence in 1966.

The current flag was adopted at the time of independence. It was the winning design in a national competition, won by Grantley Prescod, a local art teacher.

THE SYMBOLISM OF THE FLAG

Prescod interpreted the stripes as representing the blue seas and the golden sands that surround the island. The trident is adapted from the previous flag-badge which depicted Britannia holding a trident (symbolic of her rule over the seas). Here the trident is without a shaft, indicating a break with the colonial past. It is also the emblem of the sea god, Neptune, and reflects the importance of the sea to Barbados.

THE COAT OF ARMS OF BARBADOS

The coat of arms was granted by HM Queen Elizabeth II in 1966, on a visit to the island. The shield depicts a bearded fig tree, after which the island takes its name, between two "Pride of Barbados" flowers. The crest is an arm holding two sugarcanes in the form of a St. Andrew's Cross. This commemorates independence, which was achieved on St. Andrew's Day, November 30, in 1966.

Barbados also has a Governor's standard. It is the same as that of the Governor of St. Lucia *(see page 38)*, except that it bears the word "Barbados" on the scroll beneath the Royal Crest.

GRENADA

Ratio: *3:5* Adopted: *February 7, 1974* Usage: *National and Civil*

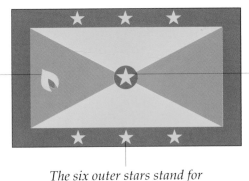

A nutmeg, Grenada's most famous product

The central star and disk represent St. George's, the capital

The six outer stars stand for the six parishes

NORTH AMERICA

St. Vincent & The Grenadines Barbados
GRENADA
Venezuela Trinidad & Tobago

FIRST SETTLED BY FRANCE, Grenada was invaded by Britain in 1762. It became an Associated State in 1967 and fully independent in 1974.

The flag used prior to independence in 1967 also featured a nutmeg, because Grenada is a major world supplier of this commodity and is known as the Spice Island.

Other features of the flag derive from the coat of arms granted on December 6, 1973, including the red, yellow, and green colors.

SYMBOLISM OF THE FLAG
The yellow star on a red disk stands for the Borough of St. George's, Grenada's capital, and the other six stars for the remaining six parishes.

In the official interpretation the red stands for courage and vitality, the yellow for wisdom and warmth, and the green for vegetation and agriculture. When the flag is used at sea its proportions are altered from 3:5 to a longer form (1:2).

THE NATIONAL ARMS
The coat of arms depicts the *Santa Maria*, Columbus' ship, a lion representing national liberty, and a lily emblem symbolizing the Virgin Mary. The shield is supported by two characteristic local creatures – an armadillo and a ramier pigeon. Beneath the shield is a representation of the Grand Etang lake, and, on a scroll at the base, what must be one of the world's longest national mottos: "Ever conscious of God we aspire, build and advance as one people."

TRINIDAD & TOBAGO

Ratio: *3:5*   Adopted: *August 31, 1962*   Usage: *National and Civil*

White
represents
the sea

Black
symbolizes
the strength
of the people

Red stands for the people

NORTH
AMERICA

Grenada TRINIDAD
&
TOBAGO

Venezuela

TRINIDAD AND TOBAGO were separate British colonies that united in 1889. They became independent in 1962 and a republic in 1976.

The flag, adopted at independence, was chosen from among designs sent in by the public. The same colors are used in the coat of arms.

A flag for Queen Elizabeth II was adopted after independence, but it became obsolete following the formation of the republic.

The President has a flag of blue with the insignia in the center. The coat of arms depicts Columbus's three ships that landed here in 1498. Beneath the ships are two golden hummingbirds. The supporters of the coat of arms are also local birds, and the whole shield stands on a scene depicting waves breaking against the rocky coasts of the islands.

Trinidad also has flags for the Prime Minister and other ministers.

THE PRESIDENT'S FLAG

The top of the shield
depicts two
hummingbirds

The scarlet ibis is one
of many local birds

The cocrico – a
local bird

In 1498 Columbus
discovered Trinidad
and his ships appear
on the shield

COLOMBIA

Ratio: 2:3   Adopted: *December 17, 1819*   Usage: *National*

The original yellow band was doubled in width when Greater Colombia was formed

Yellow recalls the federation of Greater Colombia

Blue represents independence from Spain

Red represents courage

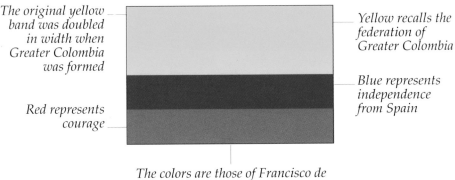

The colors are those of Francisco de Miranda, the liberation leader

SOUTH AMERICA

FOLLOWING YEARS of Spanish rule, Colombia became part of independent Greater Colombia in 1819, and then a separate republic in 1830.

The flag of Greater Colombia, adopted in 1819, was retained by Colombia after independence in 1830. For a while the stripes were arranged vertically, but the original version was restored in 1861.

There are two variant flags. The civil ensign has a red-bordered, blue oval bearing a white star in the center, used to distinguish it from the flag of Ecuador. The state flag and naval ensign have the arms in the center.

THE NATIONAL ARMS
The coat of arms dates from 1834. It includes a pomegranate, the symbol of Granada in Spain, after which the area was once named.

ARMS OF COLOMBIA

The crest is a condor, frequently used in South American heraldry

The Cap of Liberty

A map of the Isthmus of Panama

The national motto – Libertad y Orden – meaning "Liberty and Order"

A pomegranate recalls New Granada, Colombia's name when a Spanish colony

VENEZUELA

Ratio: *2:3*   Adopted: *April 20, 1836*   Usage: *National and Civil*

Blue represents
Venezuela's
independence
from Spain

Stars represent the
seven provinces
that supported
independence

Red symbolizes
courage

The flag is most similar to
that of liberation leader
Francisco de Miranda

SOUTH
AMERICA

VENEZUELA WAS once part of the Spanish province of New Granada. It then joined Greater Colombia from 1819 until independence in 1830.

The Venezuelan flag was the invention of Francisco de Miranda, who initiated the freedom of New Granada in 1806. At that time it had no stars; they were added in 1836 to symbolize the provinces that had supported the Declaration of Independence in 1811. The original plain tricolor was altered in 1819, to make the yellow double width, for use as the flag of Greater Colombia.

After independence in 1836, the flag reverted to stripes of equal width, and the stars were added.

The coat of arms dates from the 19th century but has altered frequently, especially the inscription. The present form dates from 1953.

ARMS OF VENEZUELA

The wheatsheaf
represents fertility

A running horse
symbolizes liberty

The arms appear in the
canton of the state flag
and naval ensign

Two horns of plenty
symbolize abundance

The flag and weapons
represent independence

The name of the state,
"Republica de
Venezuela"

GUYANA

Ratio: 3:5   Adopted: *May 20, 1966*   Usage: *National and Civil*

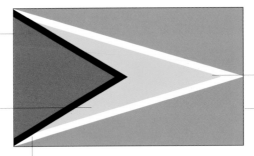

Red recalls the people's dynamism and zeal for reform

The "Golden Arrow" represents a bright future

Yellow is symbolic of mineral wealth

Green recalls the vast forests and fields

The white and black fimbriations were added by the College of Arms

SOUTH AMERICA

Venezuela
GUYANA
Suriname
Brazil

GUYANA WAS ACQUIRED by the UK in 1814. It became independent in 1966 and a republic within the UK Commonwealth in 1970.

The flag is known as the "Golden Arrow" because of the arrowhead that flies across the green field. The original design had a red field, but this was altered by the College of Arms in 1966, which also added the black and white fimbriations.

The green and yellow stand for natural resources and the red for the "zeal and dynamism [of the inhabitants] in building the nation."

THE PRESIDENT'S STANDARD
Adopted in 1970, it is a banner of the arms granted in 1966. It depicts a green shield in the center charged with an Indian crown in gold, a Victoria lily and a native pheasant.

THE PRESIDENT'S STANDARD

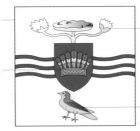

The President's flag was adopted in 1970; it is a square banner of the arms

Crown of a cacique, or Indian chief

A Victoria regia *water lily, growing from stylized heraldic water*

A native canje *pheasant*

SURINAME

Ratio: *2:3*   Adopted: *November 25, 1975*   Usage: *National and Civil*

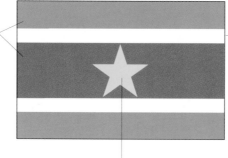

Green and red were the colors of the political parties at the time of independence

The white fimbriations represent justice and freedom

The star is an emblem of unity and hope

SOUTH AMERICA

SURINAME WAS PART of the Dutch kingdom until 1975. Since independence, there have been a series of coups and changes of constitution.

The flag was chosen in 1975 by a parliamentary commission, on the basis of designs sent in by the public. The object was to choose a flag that harmonized the colors of the main political groups (green and red) into a design suggestive of unity and progress. The star is thus the emblem of unity and hope for the future, and the white fimbriations, separating the red and green, stand for justice and freedom.

THE PRESIDENT'S STANDARD
This has a white panel in place of the star and contains the state arms. The coat of arms dates back to the 17th century and the time of Dutch rule, but was revised in 1959 and again in 1975.

THE PRESIDENT'S STANDARD

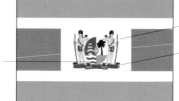

On the shield a ship reflects commerce, a diamond, mining, and a tree, agriculture

The supporters are Indians

The national motto – Justitia, Pietas, Fides meaning "Justice, Peace, Faith"

ECUADOR

Ratio: *1:2* Adopted: *September 26, 1860* Usage: *National*

Yellow is the color of federation

Red symbolizes courage

Blue, red, and yellow are the colors of Francisco de Miranda

Blue recalls independence from Spain

SOUTH AMERICA

ECUADOR, formerly a Spanish colony, joined the state of Greater Colombia in 1822. It seceded from the federation in 1830 to form a republic.

The 1819 flag of Greater Colombia was restored in Ecuador in 1860, and since then the flags of Ecuador and Colombia have been very similar. The national arms was added to the center of the basic civil flag in 1900, creating a distinct flag for national and state purposes. The civil flag on land and sea does not contain the arms, making it almost identical to the flag of Colombia, except for its proportions. When used abroad, the flag always contains the arms.

ARMS OF ECUADOR
The coat of arms dates from 1845 and depicts Mount Chimborazo and the mouth of the River Guyas.

ARMS OF ECUADOR

Four signs of the Zodiac represent the months from March to May

An allegorical scene depicts Mount Chimborazo, South America's highest peak

An Andean condor symbolizes bravery and liberty

A ship at the mouth of the River Guyas represents commerce

The ax and fasces are symbols of republicanism

PERU

Ratio: *2:3*   Adopted: *February 25, 1825*   Usage: *National and Civil*

The colors also recall those of the Incas, who ruled much of Peru until European colonization

Red and white are the colors chosen by San Martín, "El Liberador" (the Liberator)

SOUTH
AMERICA

PERU WAS FREED from Spanish rule in 1819 by an army led by José de San Martín. Since 1824 it has been an independent unitary republic.

The colors chosen by San Martín for the Peruvian Legion were red and white, said to be the colors of the Inca Empire, and the rising sun, also dating back to the Incas. The flag assumed its present form, dropping the sun, in 1825 at the behest of Simón Bolívar, another famous liberator. As is usual in former Spanish colonies, the official flag, used by the government and the armed forces, has the coat of arms in the center.

The coat of arms dates from 1825 and depicts a cornucopia, a *chichona* tree, and a llama, surrounded by state flags. The flags do not appear on the arms placed on the official flag.

ARMS OF PERU

On the coat of arms, the wreaths are substituted for national flags

A llama

A chichona tree

A cornucopia symbolizing prosperity

This is how the coat of arms appears in the center of the official flag and ensign

BRAZIL

Ratio: *7:10*   Adopted: *November 15, 1889*   Usage: *National and Civil*

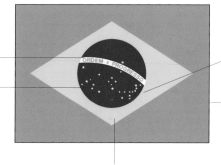

The national motto meaning "Order and Progress"

The most recent stars were added to the Canis Major constellation

Each star represents a state in the Federation

Green recalls the Brazilian rainforest

Yellow represents the country's mineral resources

SOUTH AMERICA

BRAZIL BELONGED TO Portugal until 1822, when it became an independent kingdom, and later an empire. It formed a federal republic in 1889.

The green field and yellow lozenge were part of the flag adopted in 1822 when independence was first achieved and the empire was declared. In 1889, the imperial arms was replaced by a view of the night sky as it appeared over Rio de Janeiro when the republic was formed. Each of the stars in the constellation represents a state of the Federation, including the Federal District. These have been altered from time to time, most recently in 1992 when the number of stars increased to 27.

THE CONSTELLATIONS
The constellations on the flag are represented in a realistic manner,

with stars of varying sizes, although the size of star does not reflect the importance of the state. In 1992, new stars were added to the constellation of *Canis Major* in the lower left section of the sky. The country's national motto, *Ordem e Progresso* meaning "Order and Progress," appears on a band across the center of the night sky.

THE NATIONAL CAPITAL
In Brasília, the capital since 1960, stands one of the world's tallest flagpoles, on which flies an enormous national flag.
   Brazil also has flags for the President, the Ministry of Marine, and a naval Jack.

Brazil – State flags

MANY OF THE FLAGS recall historical events or the formation of the federal republic. The date of accession is given below the state name.

THE FEDERAL DISTRICT
1960

The flag of the Federal District dates from 1969. The green rectangle contains four arrows representing the balance of centralization and devolution in Brazil.

ACRE
1962

Adopted by the republic declared in 1899, when Acre was still part of Bolivia, the flag was retained by the state, and the star was added to recall its joining the Federation.

ALAGOAS
1889

Based on the flag of 1894, this new version was instituted in 1963. In the center is the arms, also originally dating back to 1894. It recalls various aspects of the state's industry.

AMAPÁ
1989

The flag was adopted in 1984 for the territory and retained for the state. It uses all the national colors, together with an outline of the fortress of Macapá, the state capital.

AMAZONAS
1889

The flag dates from the local uprising of 1897. The stars stand for the 25 municipalities, with the large one for Manaus, the state capital. The flag was regularized in 1982.

BAHIA
1889

The flag dates back to the uprisings of 1789 and 1798, which are recalled by the white triangle. The flag in this form was first adopted in 1889, when Bahia joined the Federation.

CEARÁ
1889

The flag was instituted in 1922 and is very similar to the national flag. The arms depicts an allegorical landscape surrounded by stars. It dates from 1897 and was revised in 1967.

ESPÍRITO SANTO
1889

The flag was created in 1947. The Portuguese motto – meaning "Work and Trust" – is that of the Jesuits, and the pink and blue represent the local evening sky.

GOIÁS
1889

The flag is based on those promoted for the republic in 1889. This version has five stars for the Southern Cross, similar to those in the national arms.

MARANHÃO
1889

The flag, adopted in 1889, features the star which represents the state on the national flag, while the stripes stand for its ethnic mix.

MATO GROSSO
1889

The flag is based on the national flag, but with local interpretations of the color arrangement and one star for the state. It was adopted in 1890.

MATO GROSSO
DO SUL
1977

The design emerged from a competition held in 1978, after the new state was formed. The flag was instituted in 1979.

MINAS GERAIS
1889

The flag contains a Masonic triangle of the *Inconfidência Mineira* (miners revolt) of 1789, standing for equality.

PARÁ
1889

Based on a republican flag, it dates from 1898. The star is taken from the one for Pará on the national flag.

PARAÍBA
1889

The flag recalls Vargas' revolution in 1930. *Nego* ("I deny it") refers to the assassination of the state president.

PARANÁ
1889

The flag contains an emblem like the national flag, bearing the Southern Cross and name of the state.

PERNAMBUCO
1889

This is the flag of the Pernambuco revolution of 1817, which later became the flag of the state when the events of 1817 were celebrated.

PIAUÍ
1889

Based on the colors of the national flag, in this instance it has only one star, representing the state of Piauí. It was adopted in 1922.

RIO DE JANEIRO

1975

The state was reconstituted in 1975 to include the state of Guanabara. The new state took over the emblems of the former state of Rio de Janeiro.

RIO GRANDE DO NORTE

1889

Dating from 1957, the flag uses the arms granted in 1909, thus making it one of the newest flags of the original states.

RIO GRANDE DO SUL

1889

The flag dates from the revolution of 1836, which created the Republic of Rio Grande do Sul. It was readopted in 1891, and the arms were added.

RONDÔNIA

1981

Rondônia's flag uses the four national colors and a single star symbol. It was adopted in 1981 after a design competition.

RORAIMA

1989

The flag, adopted when the territory became a federal state, uses the national colors and star, with a red line representing the Equator.

SANTA CATARINA

1889

The red and white flag precedes the republic. It was most recently regularized in 1953, when the arms were placed in the center.

SÃO PAULO

1889

The flag was created in 1888 at the start of the republican revolution and revived in 1932, with 13 stripes.

SERGIPE

1889

The flag was created in the late 19th century and adopted in 1920. In 1951 the stars were repositioned.

TOCANTINS

1989

After achieving statehood, a flag and arms were adopted, using blue and white from the national colors.

CHILE

Ratio: *2:3*   Adopted: *October 18, 1817*   Usage: *National and Civil*

Blue represents
the clear
Andean skies

White
symbolizes
the snow of
the Andes

Red is for the blood
shed for freedom

The flag is modeled on the US
Stars and Stripes

SOUTH
AMERICA

CHILE WAS FREED from Spanish rule in 1818, largely through the efforts of José de San Martín, leader of the Army of the Andes.

Adopted in 1817, after San Martín's victory at Chacabuco, the national flag of Chile was preceded by at least two other versions during the early years of separatism. The current flag was based on the Stars and Stripes.

The white star was reserved for use only on the official flag until 1864, when the starred flag was made official for all purposes.

THE PRESIDENT'S STANDARD
The flag of the President is the same as the national flag, with the national arms in the center. The coat of arms dates from 1834. It is supported by an *huemal* deer and a condor. The crest is formed from the feathers of the *rhea* bird. The motto – *Por La Razon o La Fuerza* – means "By reason or by force."

THE PRESIDENT'S STANDARD

An **huemal** *deer, of the high Andes*

A crest of feathers
from the **rhea** bird

The condor is a
common symbol on
South American arms

BOLIVIA

Ratio: 2:3   Adopted: *November 30, 1851*   Usage: *National and Civil*

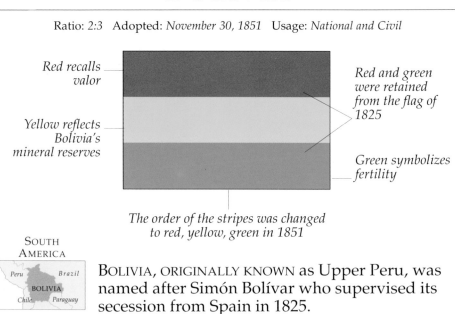

Red recalls valor

Yellow reflects Bolivia's mineral reserves

Red and green were retained from the flag of 1825

Green symbolizes fertility

The order of the stripes was changed to red, yellow, green in 1851

SOUTH AMERICA

Peru   Brazil   BOLIVIA   Chile   Paraguay

BOLIVIA, ORIGINALLY KNOWN as Upper Peru, was named after Simón Bolívar who supervised its secession from Spain in 1825.

The flag of 1825 had three stripes of red-green-red, with five gold stars within laurel wreaths. These stood for the original five departments.

A NEW TRICOLOR
In 1826, the flag was altered to three equal stripes of yellow, green, and red with the arms in the center.

It was last altered in 1851, when the order of the stripes was changed to red, yellow, green.

The official flag still has the arms in the center. It was regulated in 1888 and depicts Mount Potosí, an alpaca, a wheatsheaf, and a breadfruit tree. The oval ring contains nine stars for the nine departments.

ARMS OF BOLIVIA

As on many South American arms, the crest is a condor

The allegorical scene on the shield represents Bolivia's agricultural and industrial wealth

The flags and weapons represent the people's willingness to defend the state

The nine stars represent Bolivia's nine departments

PARAGUAY

Ratio: 3:5   Adopted: November 25, 1842   Usage: National and Civil

On the reverse, the flag is charged with the Treasury Seal

The Star of May is used as a symbol of freedom on many South American flags

The colors were influenced by the French Tricolore, which had become a symbol of liberation

SOUTH AMERICA

PARAGUAY DECLARED its independence from Spain in 1811 and has remained an independent republic ever since.

The colors of the flag and the Star of May emblem date from the Declaration of Independence. A number of variant designs existed prior to the current design, which was regularized in 1842. The current flag has a separate emblem on each side, a practice dating from the time of José de Francia, in power from 1814–40. During his regime, one side of the flag carried the arms of Spain and the other the arms of Asunción.

The current emblems, adopted in 1821, but not officially sanctioned until 1842, are the national arms on the front (obverse) and the Treasury Seal on the back (reverse).

STATE ARMS ON THE OBVERSE

The Star of May recalls the date of independence

Name of the state

TREASURY SEAL ON THE REVERSE

The Cap of Liberty guarded by a lion

PAZ Y JUSTICIA

The state motto – Paz y Justicia ("Peace and Justice")

URUGUAY

Ratio: 2:3   Adopted: *July 11, 1830*   Usage: *National and Civil*

The Sun of May has been a national emblem since the 19th century

Blue and white are also the national colors of Argentina, from which this flag derives

The nine stripes represent the nine departments

SOUTH AMERICA

HISTORICALLY A SPANISH colony, Uruguay was annexed to Brazil and then to Argentina before becoming fully independent in 1830.

The colours, blue and white, and the Sun of May on the current flag come from the Argentinian flag.

THE FLAG OF ARTIGAS
The colors were brought to Uruguay by José Artigas, who led the movement for separation. His flag was blue and white striped, with a red diagonal. Variations of this flag remained in use after Uruguay was annexed to Brazil in 1821.

When full independence was assumed, the present form of the flag was instituted. The nine stripes represent the nine departments. The Sun of May has been used as the national emblem since 1815 and now appears as the crest on the coat of arms.

FLAG OF ARTIGAS

The colors derived from those of Argentina's flag

This flag is now used as a Jack for naval vessels

Red represents the Banda Oriental (*the "East Bank"*) of Uruguay

ARGENTINA

Ratio: *1:2*   Adopted: *February 12, 1812*   Usage: *National and Civil*

Blue and white were formed into a flag by Manuel Belgrano, the leader of the revolution

The Sun of May was added in 1818 to create a flag for state use

Blue and white recall the sky when the first uprising for independence was staged

SOUTH AMERICA

ARGENTINA ACHIEVED its independence from Spain in 1816. Liberation demonstrations began in Buenos Aires on May 25, 1810.

The colors, adopted by Manuel Belgrano, the leader of the revolution, were first used at the Battle of Rosario in 1812. They were based on the blue and white cockades adopted after the May 25 gathering when, it is said, white clouds parted to reveal the blue sky and the shining sun, inspiring the "Sun of May" emblem.

THE SUN FLAG

In 1818 the emblem and the colors were combined to form the sun flag used today as the national and official flag. The form of the sun is taken from the one depicted on the 8-*real* and 8-*escudo* coins of 1813.

The arms also used the Sun of May emblem and the national colors.

ARMS OF ARGENTINA

The Sun of May

The Cap of Liberty

A wreath of laurel

Blue and white are Argentina's national colors

MOROCCO

Ratio: 2:3   Adopted: *November 17, 1915*   Usage: *National and Civil*

Red represents the descendants of the Prophet Muhammad

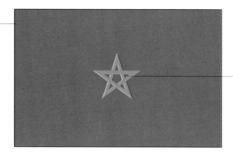

The Seal of Solomon was added in 1915

AFRICA

MOROCCO HAS BEEN independent since 1956, becoming a kingdom in 1957. The state has occupied Western Sahara since 1975.

Red has considerable historic significance in Morocco, proclaiming the descent of the royal family from the Prophet Muhammad via Fatima, the wife of Ali, the fourth Caliph. Red is also the color that was used by the Sherifs of Mecca and the Imams of Yemen.

THE SEAL OF SOLOMON

From the 17th century on, when Morocco was ruled by the Hassani Dynasty, the flags of the country were plain red. In 1915, during the reign of Mulay Yusuf, the green Seal of Solomon was added to the national flag. The Seal is an interlaced pentangle, used as a symbol in occult law for centuries.

THE COLONIAL ERA

While Morocco was under French and Spanish control, the red flag with the seal in the center remained in use – but only inland. Its use at sea was prohibited. When independence was restored in 1956, it once again became the national flag.

THE NATIONAL ARMS

After independence, in 1958, Morocco adopted a national coat of arms. This depicts the sun rising over the Atlas Mountains. The arms also includes the Seal of Solomon from the national flag. On the scroll is an inscription from the Qur'an (Koran) that reads "If you assist God, he will assist you."

ALGERIA

Ratio: 2:3   Adopted: *July 3, 1962*   Usage: *National and Civil*

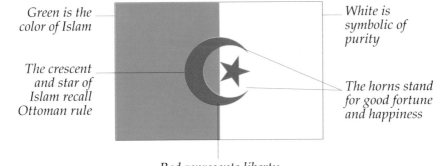

Green is the color of Islam

White is symbolic of purity

The crescent and star of Islam recall Ottoman rule

The horns stand for good fortune and happiness

Red represents liberty

AFRICA

ALGERIA WAS occupied by the French after 1830. Independence was achieved in 1962 after a long struggle led by the National Liberation Front.

The flag of Algeria was adopted by the National Liberation Front (*Front de Libération National*) in 1954, on the basis of an older design, created in 1928, by the nationalist leader Messali Hadj. From 1958–62 it was the flag of the Provisional Government in exile, but it was retained when independence was achieved in 1962 and has remained unchanged ever since.

SYMBOLISM IN THE FLAG
The green in the hoist is the traditional color of Islam, and the white represents purity. The horns of the crescent are longer than usual and represent increase or good fortune and happiness, while the whole emblem recalls the period of Ottoman rule during the 16th century; its color, red, is symbolic of liberty.

THE NAVAL ENSIGN
The naval ensign has two crossed anchors in the canton. This device is used on the naval ensigns of several Arab countries, following the example of Egypt.

THE EMBLEM OF ALGERIA
The state coat of arms is based on the well-known local emblem of the "Hand of Fatima." It also contains the crescent and star of Islam, alongside symbols reflecting both agriculture and industry.

TUNISIA

Ratio: *2:3*   Adopted: *1835*   Usage: *National and Civil*

The
crescent
and star of
Islam

Red taken
from the
flag of
Turkey

AFRICA

PART OF THE TURKISH EMPIRE until 1881, Tunisia then became a French Protectorate. In 1957, it became a republic when the Bey was deposed.

The flag is based on that of the Turkish Empire and was adopted by the Bey, the hereditary ruler of Tunisia, in 1835, primarily as a military flag. During the French administration (1881–1957) it became a sea flag, with the French *Tricolore* in the canton; this was removed when independence was achieved in 1956.

The coat of arms of Tunisia has been altered since the abolition of the monarchy, most recently in 1963, and unusually has the motto on a scroll on the shield itself. The motto reads – in Arabic – "Order, Liberty, Justice." The ship, lion, and balance were retained from the previous arms.

ARMS OF TUNISIA

The ship, lion, and balance symbolize the national motto

The ship also recalls early settlers

The national motto – "Order, Liberty, Justice"

LIBYA

Ratio: *3:5* Adopted: *1977* Usage: *National and Civil*

Green is the
national color
of Libya

It is the only
national flag
of a single
plain color

Green also reflects the
people's devotion to Islam

AFRICA

LIBYA ACHIEVED independence in 1951, but in 1969 the King was deposed, and Libya formed a republic led by Colonel Gadaffi.

The flag of the independent kingdom was red, black, and green with a crescent and star in the center, but after the revolution of 1969, the flag became three simple stripes of red, white, and black.

In 1971, Libya joined the Federation of Arab Republics with Egypt and Syria, which used a similar flag with a hawk emblem in the center and the name of the country beneath it.

When Libya left the Federation in 1977, the new plain green flag was adopted. The national emblem remains similar to the one used while Libya was part of the Federation, which shows the Hawk of Quraish.

ARMS OF LIBYA

The Hawk of Quraish is
the emblem of the tribe
of Muhammad

The title of the
state – "The
Great Socialist
People's Libyan
Arab Republic"

EGYPT

Ratio: *2:3*   Adopted: *October 4, 1984*   Usage: *National and Civil*

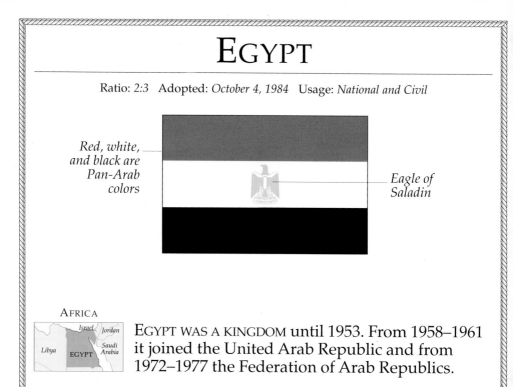

Red, white, and black are Pan-Arab colors

Eagle of Saladin

AFRICA

Israel *Jordan*
Libya **EGYPT** *Saudi Arabia*

EGYPT WAS A KINGDOM until 1953. From 1958–1961 it joined the United Arab Republic and from 1972–1977 the Federation of Arab Republics.

As a kingdom, the flag was green with a white crescent and three stars.

THE UNITED ARAB REPUBLIC
When the United Arab Republic (UAR) was formed in 1958, they adapted the flag of the Liberation Rally that led the independence revolt of 1952–53. The UAR flag was red, white, and black, with two green stars in the center of the white stripe. In 1972, when the Federation was formed, the stars were replaced with the Hawk of the Quraish (*see page 61*), in gold above the state name.

In 1984, Egypt reverted to the gold eagle used by the Liberation Rally. These colors and the eagle emblem have been widely copied in other Arab countries.

FLAG OF THE
LIBERATION RALLY
1952–58

The gold eagle is said to be the Eagle of Saladin

The crescent and stars were retained from the old national flag

SUDAN

Ratio: *1:2*   Adopted: *May 20, 1970*   Usage: *National and Civil*

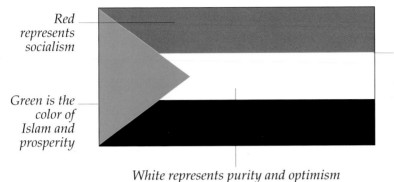

Red — represents socialism

Green is the — color of Islam and prosperity

Red, white, — black, and green are Pan-Arab colors

White represents purity and optimism

AFRICA

RULED JOINTLY by Egypt and Britain from 1877, Sudan became independent in 1956. Since then it has had a series of different regimes.

The flag used at independence was a horizontal tricolor of blue, yellow, and green, but following the formation of the Democratic Republic in 1968, a new flag was chosen by competition.

A PAN-ARAB FLAG
This is very similar to the flags of other Arab countries, with the green

as a triangle in the hoist. White is believed to represent purity and optimism, red stands for socialism, and green for prosperity.

In 1969 a new coat of arms was adopted, with a secretary bird bearing a shield from the time of the Mahdi, (who briefly ruled Sudan in the 19th century). Two scrolls are placed above and below the secretary bird.

ARMS OF SUDAN

The title of the state – Al-Jamhuriya as-Sudaniya ("Republic of Sudan")

The national motto – Al-nasr lina ("Victory is ours")

A secretary bird bears the shield

ERITREA

Ratio: 2:3   Adopted: *May 24, 1993*   Usage: *National and Civil*

An olive branch is encircled by a wreath representing Eritrean autonomy

Green, blue, and red are the colors of the Eritrean People's Liberation Front

ERITREA WAS FEDERATED to Ethiopia in 1952 and fully integrated in 1962. Beginning in 1972, a long war of secession led to independence in 1993.

The flag of the Eritrean People's Liberation Front (EPLF), which campaigned for independence, is green and blue with a red triangle bearing a gold star. The flag adopted on independence retained the colors and pattern but replaced the star with the emblem used previously for autonomous Eritrea. This is an olive branch surrounded by a wreath of olive leaves. Originally this emblem was green on a blue flag, but it is now yellow.

THE PRESIDENT'S FLAG

The President's flag contains the national coat of arms, which depicts a camel in a desert, with the name of the state underneath in English, Tigrinya and Arabic.

THE PRESIDENT'S FLAG

The arms of Eritrea

The coat of arms is surrounded by a wreath of leaves

The colors of the national flag are used

DJIBOUTI

Ratio: 21:38   Adopted: *June 27, 1977*   Usage: *National and Civil*

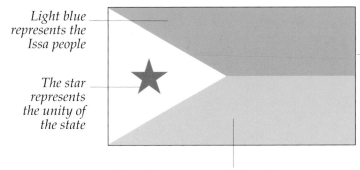

Light blue represents the Issa people

The star represents the unity of the state

White, green, and light blue are the colors of the LPAI

Green represents the Afar people, with their land and links to Islam

Eritrea Yemen DJIBOUTI Ethiopia Somalia

ONCE KNOWN AS FRENCH SOMALILAND, and after 1967 as the Territory of the Afars and Issas, Djibouti gained independence in 1977.

The national flag adopted in 1977 was an adaptation of the flag of the *Ligue Populaire Africaine pour l'Indépendance* (LPAI) that led Djibouti to independence. The LPAI flag had a red triangle with a white star. For the national flag, adopted at independence, the star was placed in an upright rather than a slanted position, and the proportions of the flag were lengthened. The colors signify the Issas and the Afars, the two peoples of Djibouti at independence, and the red star signifies the unity of the diverse state.

The coat of arms is centered around a local Somali shield and spear, bordered by two hunting knives.

ARMS OF DJIBOUTI

A Somali shield and weapons; two hunting knives and a spear

The red star is a traditional symbol of unity

The coat of arms contains a local shield

ETHIOPIA

Ratio: *1:2*   Adopted: *February 6, 1996*   Usage: *National and Civil*

The emblem represents diversity and unity

Yellow is the color of peace and love

Green recalls the land and hope for the future

The colors date back to the 19th century

Red is symbolic of strength

AFRICA

ETHIOPIA WAS RECOGNIZED as an empire in the 19th century. It was occupied by Italy from 1936–41. The Emperor was overthrown in 1974.

The three traditional colors – green, yellow, and red – date back to the Emperor Menelik (1889–1913) and were first used in a flag in 1895.

The current flag and emblem were adopted after the defeat of the Marxist Mengistu regime, in power from 1974–1991. The emblem is intended to represent both the diversity and unity of the country.

ETHIOPIA AND THE RASTAFARI
In the 1930s the Ethiopian colors became popular with black activists in Jamaica who looked to Ethiopia for political and spiritual guidance. Since then, these colors (along with black from the flag of Marcus Garvey [*see page 7*]) have become linked with the Rastafarian movement, and have spread to other African countries.

EMBLEM OF ETHIOPIA

The star represents diversity and unity

Blue represents peace

The sun's rays symbolize prosperity

SOMALIA

Ratio: *2:3*   Adopted: *October 12, 1954*   Usage: *National and Civil*

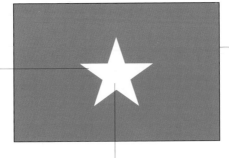

The five-pointed star represents the branches of the Somali race; in Ethiopia, Kenya, Djibouti, and the former British and Italian colonies

The blue is the same as that used by the United Nations

The star of unity

MODERN SOMALIA is a combination of the former Italian territory and British Somaliland. Since 1991 it has been in a state of civil war.

The flag was adopted by the Italian Trusteeship Territory in 1954 on the basis of the blue and white flag of the United Nations, which was supervising the territory at the time. It was retained when Somalia became independent in 1960. The five-pointed star is said to stand for the five branches of the Somali race, including those living in Ethiopia, Djibouti and Kenya.

ARMS OF SOMALIA
The coat of arms was adopted in 1956. The leopards that support the shield and the white star were also found on the arms used during the Italian administration.

ARMS OF SOMALIA

The shield is based on the national flag

Below the shield are two palm branches and two spears

The supporters are leopards; a leopard also featured on the shield of the colonial arms

UGANDA

Ratio: *2:3*   Adopted: *October 9, 1962*   Usage: *National and Civil*

The colors of the flag represent the Ugandan people, sunlight, and brotherhood

The great crested crane is the national badge of Uganda

Black, yellow, and red are the party colors of the UPC

AFRICA

SINCE INDEPENDENCE in 1962, Uganda has suffered years of upheaval. Under the current regime some stability has been restored.

The dominant party at the time of independence was the Uganda People's Congress (UPC), and the new national flag was an adaptation of its tricolor with the addition of the crane badge in the center. This dates back to before independence when the colonial badge of Uganda was the great crested crane. It also appears as one of the supporters on

Uganda's coat of arms granted on September 3, 1962. The arms depicts a local shield, in an allegorical landscape with tea and cotton plants.

THE PRESIDENT'S STANDARD
The flag for the President was adopted in 1963 and consists of the arms on a red field with the national colors along the lower edge.

THE PRESIDENT'S STANDARD

A deer is one of the supporters

Tea and cotton are Uganda's most important crops

A great crested crane supports the shield

Blue and white represent the waters of the Nile and of Lake Victoria

KENYA

Ratio: *2:3*   Adopted: *December 12, 1963*   Usage: *National and Civil*

Black, red, and green are *KANU* party colors

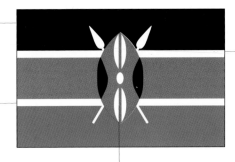

The white fimbriations were added to the *KANU* flag to create the national flag

White was added to represent the democratic party

The African shield is also used in the national arms

AFRICA

KENYA BECAME a colony in 1920 having previously been known as British East Africa. It became independent in 1963 and a republic in 1964.

The flag adopted at independence was based on that of the Kenya Africa National Union (KANU); the dominant political party. For the national flag, white fimbriations were added, and the shield and spears were redrawn.

A coat of arms was adopted in 1963 and makes use of the same shield and spears but with a white cock in the center, grasping an ax.

Kenya was the first African country to use a shield of traditional design in its coat of arms, a practice which has since been followed in many other new states. It was also the first to give the motto in a local language, in this case Swahili.

ARMS OF KENYA

The shield stands on a representation of Mount Kenya

The cock with an ax is the *KANU* party symbol

Harambee meaning "Pull Together" in Swahili

RWANDA

Ratio: *6:13*   Adopted: *31 December 2001*   Usage: *National and Civil*

Light blue
stands for
the hope
of happiness
and peace

The Golden Sun
symbolizes the
enlightenment
that will bring
unity and fight
ignorance

Yellow is
symbolic of
the need for
economic
growth

Green represents
future prosperity

AFRICA

RWANDA, originally part of German East Africa, was taken over by Belgium after World War I. It became independent on July 1, 1962.

In 2001 Rwanda adopted a new national flag, national arms, and a national anthem, in response to the government's desire to concentrate on future possibilities rather than the troubled past. It was decided that the old national symbols reinforced the ideas of ethnic separatism and violence which eventually led to the genocide of 1994. For the new flag, red and black, which have often been associated with blood and mourning respectively, were removed, in favor of the more optimistic blue, yellow, and green. The new national symbols of Rwanda signify national unity, respect for work, patriotism, and confidence in the future.

THE NATIONAL FLAG 1961–2001

'R' stands for
Rwanda

Red, yellow,
and green are
pan-African
colors

BURUNDI

Ratio: 2:3   Adopted: *June 28, 1967*   Usage: *National and Civil*

Red is symbolic
of blood shed in
the struggle for
independence

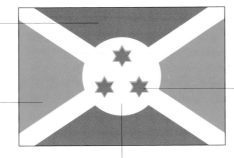

The three stars
represent the
three ethnic
groups; the
Tutsi, Hutu,
and Twa

Green
represents
hope

White signifies peace

AFRICA

LIKE RWANDA, Burundi was a German, then a
Belgian territory. It achieved independence as a
kingdom in 1962 and became a republic in 1966.

The flag adopted at independence
had a drum – symbolic of the
monarchy – and a sorghum plant in
the central disk. When the kingdom
was abolished the drum was
removed, and a year later the
sorghum plant was replaced by the
three stars, said to symbolize the
three ethnic groups.

THE NATIONAL ARMS
The coat of arms has also been
altered. The royal drum, which was
above the shield was removed, a
more republican motto was adopted,
and the four spears were reduced to
three, again to represent the ethnic
groups. The golden lion's face also
featured on the royal badge.

ARMS OF BURUNDI

Three spears represent
Burundi's ethnic groups

The lion's face has
remained unchanged
since the original
coat of arms was
adopted in 1962

The motto is Unite-
Travail-Progres
meaning "Unity,
Work, Progress"

CENTRAL AFRICAN REPUBLIC

Ratio: 2:3   Adopted: December 1, 1958   Usage: National and Civil

The star represents hope of a union under France

Red, white, and blue are taken from the French Tricolore

Red, yellow, and green are Pan-African colors

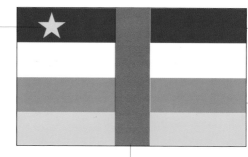

The vertical stripe represents unity and the blood of humanity

PREVIOUSLY KNOWN AS Ubangui-Shari, the Central African Republic was formed as an autonomous state in 1958 under French protection.

The flag is unique in that it combines the Pan-African colors with those of France, the former colonial power. This was done in the hope that neighboring states would join a federation under French protection, but this never materialized; the star represents the hope of achieving this goal. The state became an empire under the Emperor Bokassa from 1976–79, but no change was made to the national symbols.

The coat of arms symbolizes both the Central African Republic and its important position in the center of Africa. The upper scroll bears the motto of the former ruling party; it means "A Man is a Man."

ARMS OF THE CENTRAL AFRICAN REPUBLIC

An elephant and a baobab tree

The national motto – Unité, Dignité, Travail meaning "Unity, Dignity, Work"

The central feature is a gold star on a map of Africa, symbolizing the position of the Central African Republic

The hand was the emblem of the dominant party in 1963, when the arms was adopted

DEM. REP. CONGO (ZAIRE)

Ratio: *2:3*   Adopted: *May 17, 1997*   Usage: *National and Civil*

The six stars represent the six original provinces of Dem. Rep. Congo (Zaire) in 1960

A blue flag with a yellow star was the flag of the Congo Free State from 1877–1908

AFRICA

THE DEMOCRATIC REPUBLIC OF THE CONGO, known as Zaire from 1971 to 1997, gained independence in 1960. It has yet to achieve political stability.

The current flag of Dem. Rep. Congo (Zaire) was readopted on the May 17, 1997, following a successful *coup d'etat* by rebel forces.

THE MPR FLAG
Prior to the coup, the flag of Zaire was based on the party flag of the *Movement Populaire de la Révolution* (MPR) who came to power in 1971.

THE FLAGS OF 1960–1971
The current flag was first adopted at independence from Belgium in 1960. In 1963, it was replaced by a blue flag with a single yellow star in the canton and a yellow bordered, red stripe running diagonally. It is believed that the new leader of Congo (Zaire), Laurent Kabila, may revert to the flag of 1963.

FLAG OF CONGO-KINSHASA 1963–1971

This flag was adopted on July 1, 1963. It was the national flag until 1971.

NIGER

Ratio: *2:3*   Adopted: *November 23, 1959*   Usage: *National and Civil*

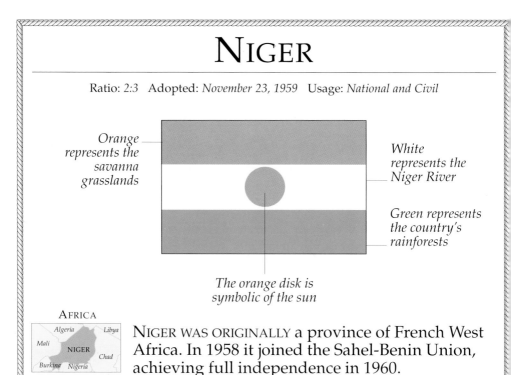

Orange represents the savanna grasslands

White represents the Niger River

Green represents the country's rainforests

The orange disk is symbolic of the sun

AFRICA

Algeria   *Libya*
Mali   NIGER   *Chad*
Burkina *Nigeria*

NIGER WAS ORIGINALLY a province of French West Africa. In 1958 it joined the Sahel-Benin Union, achieving full independence in 1960.

The flag was designed in 1958 with that of the Ivory Coast, with which Niger was in alliance, along with Chad and Dahomey (modern Benin). This alliance came to nothing, but flags were adopted that indicated their common interest. In the case of Niger, the orange is said to stand for the savanna and the green for the rainforest, while the white strip stands for the Niger River, and the orange disk for the sun. The flag was retained on independence and has remained unchanged ever since.

Four flags appear on the arms of Niger, surrounding a green shield. On the shield are weapons, the sun, a corn cob, and a buffalo's head.

ARMS OF NIGER

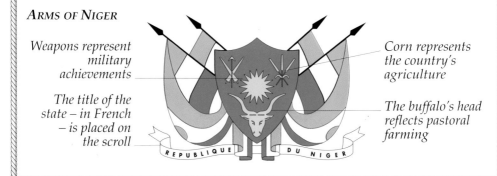

Weapons represent military achievements

The title of the state – in French – is placed on the scroll

Corn represents the country's agriculture

The buffalo's head reflects pastoral farming

REPUBLIQUE   DU NIGER

CHAD

Ratio: 2:3   Adopted: *November 6, 1959*   Usage: *National and Civil*

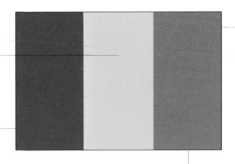

Yellow symbolizes the sun and deserts

Blue symbolizes the sky and waters of the south

The flag combines two Pan-African colors – red and yellow, with two colors from the French Tricolore – blue and red

Red recalls the blood shed for independence

AFRICA

CHAD BECAME AN autonomous republic in 1958 and for two years joined with Niger, Ivory Coast, and Dahomey in the informal Sahel-Benin Union.

The flag is a combination of the Pan-African colors popularized by Ghana, and those of the French *Tricolore*, on which it is closely modeled. It was adopted for the autonomous republic and retained on independence in 1960. Despite many upheavals since independence the flag has not been changed.

THE NATIONAL ARMS

The coat of arms dates from 1970, although Chad also has a seal (like many former French colonies), adopted in 1959. The colors are those of the national flag and the shield is supported by a lion and a wild goat. The medal below the shield is the badge of the National Order of Chad.

ARMS OF CHAD

The red symbol is for salt, the country's main mineral

A mountain goat represents the north of Chad

The wavy bars symbolize Lake Chad

The lion is symbolic of the south of the country

The national motto – Unite, Travail, Progres ("Unity, Work, Progress")

75

MAURITANIA

Ratio: *2:3* Adopted: *April 1, 1959* Usage: *National and Civil*

Green also recalls the country's Islamic faith

The crescent and star of Islam

Yellow and green are both Pan-African colors

AFRICA

MAURITANIA BECAME fully independent from France in 1960. From 1976–79 on it occupied part of Western Sahara now occupied by Morocco.

The flag was adopted in 1959 for the autonomous republic. It consists simply of a yellow crescent and star of Islam on a green field, expressive of the country's full title – "The Mauritanian Islamic Republic."

Mauritania also has seal, like those used in many former French colonies. It is uncolored and represents a genuine seal, used for certifying documents.

It bears the title of the state around the edge. In the center are the Islamic crescent and star emblems. These are decorated with a palm branch and a millet plant, both important national plants. The seal was adopted for Mauritania in 1960.

SEAL OF MAURITANIA

The name of the country is given in both French and Arabic

A palm branch

The star and crescent of Islam

A millet plant

MALI

Ratio: *2:3* Adopted: *March 1, 1961* Usage: *National and Civil*

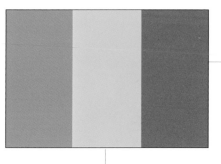

Green, yellow, and red are Pan-African colors

The style of the flag is modeled on the French Tricolore

AFRICA

MALI ACHIEVED INDEPENDENCE from France in confederation with Senegal on June 20, 1960, but split away later the same year to form a republic.

The flag adopted in 1959 for the Confederation was an imitation of the flag of Ghana, but following the style of the French *Tricolore*. It was charged with a black emblem known as a *kanaga*, a stylized human figure. The colors were intended to reflect a unity with other African nations.

After the two countries split up in 1960, the flag was kept for use in Mali until March 1, 1961, when the black figure was dropped.

Mali also has a seal, like those of other former French colonies. It is uncolored and displays a local fortress between two bows and arrows. Above the fortress is a dove of peace and below it is a rising sun.

SEAL OF MALI

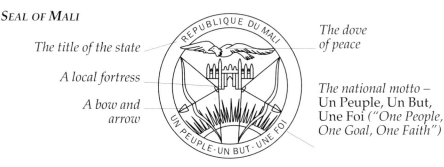

The title of the state

A local fortress

A bow and arrow

The dove of peace

The national motto – Un Peuple, Un But, Une Foi (*"One People, One Goal, One Faith"*)

SENEGAL

Ratio: *2:3*   Adopted: *September 1960*   Usage: *National and Civil*

The Pan-
African colors:
red, yellow,
and green

The design is
modeled on a
French
Tricolore

The star represents unity and hope

AFRICA

SENEGAL ACHIEVED independence from France in federation with Mali in June 1960. The Federation lasted until August 1960.

The original flag for the Federation with Mali was adopted on April 4, 1959. It remained in use in Mali until March 1961.

A NEW NATIONAL FLAG
After the breakup of the Federation in 1960, Senegal adopted a new national flag; and changed the black

kanaga emblem on the original Federation flag to a green star. This has remained the flag ever since.

The coat of arms was designed by a French heraldist in 1965. It depicts a rampant lion and a baobab tree – emblems that had appeared on earlier badges of Senegal. The medal is the star of the National Order.

ARMS OF SENEGAL

*The lion and baobab
tree appeared on
previous arms*

*A wreath of palm
branches*

*The star of the
National Order*

*The star is the
same as on the
national flag*

*The motto is the same
as Mali's – Un Peuple,
Un But, Une Foi ("One
People, One Goal,
One Faith")*

GAMBIA

Ratio: *2:3*   Adopted: *February 18, 1965*   Usage: *National and Civil*

Red represents the savanna grasslands

The blue stripe symbolizes the River Gambia

Green symbolizes the forests

AFRICA

THE GAMBIA BECAME self-governing in 1963 and fully independent of Britain on February 18, 1965. It became a republic on April 24, 1970.

The flag of the Gambia has no political basis. The blue stripe of the flag represents the River Gambia flowing between the green forest and the red savanna. It was adopted at independence in 1965.

The coat of arms was granted before independence, in 1964. It makes no reference to the previous colonial badge of the Gambia and follows traditional heraldry. The two tools represent the main ethnic groups – the Mandinka and the Fulani – and the crest, above the helmet, is a local oil palm.

The federation formed with Senegal from 1981–1989 had no effect on the national symbols.

ARMS OF THE GAMBIA

The supporters are two lions, shown holding tools

The national motto – "Progress, Peace, Prosperity"

A crest of oil palm leaves

An ax and a hoe represent the Mandinka and the Fulani, the two main ethnic groups in The Gambia

CAPE VERDE

Ratio: *10:17*   Adopted: *February 25, 1992*   Usage: *National and Civil*

The ten stars stand for the ten islands of Cape Verde

The red stripe between the white represents the road to progress

Blue represents the Atlantic Ocean

AFRICA

CAPE VERDE WAS originally an overseas province of Portugal. It obtained independence in 1975. In 1992 a multiparty constitution was adopted.

The flag adopted in 1975 was very similar to that of Guinea-Bissau, as both were based on the flag of the same dominant political party.

The current flag, adopted by the new government in 1992, depicts the ocean in blue, with the islands as a ring of stars on a line of red fimbriated in white, representing the road to progress. The stars may be derived from the arms of Praia, the capital.

The national arms depicts a torch on a triangle, symbolizing unity and freedom. It also includes the ring of stars and a plumb bob signifying rectitude and virtue, which are the "keystones" of the Constitution.

ARMS OF CAPE VERDE

The title of the state

The stars represent the main islands of Cape Verde

The plumb bob is symbolic of rectitude and virtue

The torch and triangle represent unity and freedom

GUINEA-BISSAU

Ratio: 1:2   Adopted: *September 24, 1973*   Usage: *National and Civil*

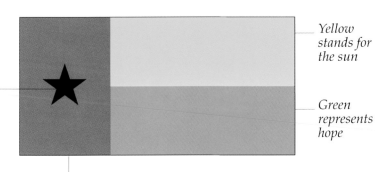

The black star represents the unity of Africa

Yellow stands for the sun

Green represents hope

Red stands for the blood shed during the struggle for independence

AFRICA

GUINEA-BISSAU is so-called to distinguish it from French Guinea. Formerly a territory of Portugal, Guinea-Bissau achieved self-government in 1973.

Like the former flag of Cape Verde, the flag is based on that of the *Partido Africano para a Independencia da Guiné e Cabo Verde* (PAIGC), still the dominant party in Guinea-Bissau.

THE GHANAIAN INFLUENCE

The party flag was derived from that of Ghana, which first used the Pan-African combination of red, yellow, green, and black in 1957. In the Ghanaian view, the black star stands for the unity of Africa. The colors represent the blood shed for independence, hope, and the sun – the source of life.

The coat of arms is the PAIGC badge, a black star, and a scallop shell.

ARMS OF GUINEA-BISSAU

A star symbolizing African unity

The PAIGC motto – Unidade, Luta, Progresso *meaning* "Unity, Struggle, Progress"

As the PAIGC badge, the palm leaves represented Guinea-Bissau

The scallop shell originally recalled the Cape Verde islands

GUINEA

Ratio: *2:3*   Adopted: *November 10, 1958*   Usage: *National and Civil*

Yellow represents
the sun and the
riches of the earth

Green represents
the country's
vegetation

The flag is
modeled on the
French Tricolore,
but in Pan-
African colors

Red symbolizes the people's sacrifice

AFRICA

Senegal
Guinea-Bissau
Sierra Leone
Mali
GUINEA
Ivory Coast

IN 1958, GUINEA became the first territory in former French West Africa to gain independence without first becoming an autonomous republic.

The colors of the flag were adapted from those of the *Rassemblement Démocratique Africaine*, the dominant movement at the time of independence. Their colors were in turn derived from those of Ghana, which had first adopted them in 1957. Sekour Touré, the first President of Guinea, was a close associate of Kwame Nkrumah, the former dictator of Ghana.

ARMS OF GUINEA
The coat of arms has been altered since the fall of Sekour Touré. The elephant's head was dropped and it now portrays a dove above an olive branch and crossed weapons.

ARMS OF GUINEA

The weapons recall
periods of war

The olive branch
symbolizes peace

The dove is a
symbol of peace

The national motto
Travail, Justice,
Solidarité, *meaning*
"Work, Justice,
Solidarity"

TRAVAIL   JUSTICE   SOLIDARITÉ

SIERRA LEONE

Ratio: *2:3*   Adopted: *April 27, 1961*   Usage: *National and Civil*

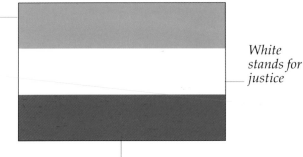

Green represents the agricultural and natural resources of the country

White stands for justice

Blue recalls the natural harbor at Freetown, the capital

AFRICA

SIERRA LEONE was founded as a home for freed slaves in 1787 but became a British colony in 1808. It achieved independence in 1961.

The arms and flag of Sierra Leone were devised by the College of Arms and granted in 1960.

ARMS OF SIERRA LEONE
The shield depicts a lion beneath a zigzag border, representing the Lion Mountains after which the territory was named, and three torches. At the base are wavy bars depicting the sea. The supporters are lions, similar to those on the colonial badge.

The three main colors from the shield – green, white, and blue – were used to form the flag. They represent agricultural and natural resources in green, unity and justice in white, and blue for the harbor at Freetown.

ARMS OF SIERRA LEONE

The torches symbolize education and progress

National motto – "Unity, Freedom, Justice"

The lions holding oil palms are taken from the old colonial badge

The border represents the Lion Mountains

The wavy bars depict the sea

LIBERIA

Ratio: *10:19*   Adopted: *July 26, 1847*   Usage: *National and Civil*

The star represents African freedom

The flag is modeled on the US Stars and Stripes

11 stripes represent the men who signed the Liberian Declaration of Independence

AFRICA

Sierra Leone · Guinea · Ivory Coast · LIBERIA

LIBERIA WAS FOUNDED in 1816 by the American Colonization Society as a home for freed slaves from the US. It became independent in 1847.

The flag of Liberia is clearly based on that of the US. Its one white star in a blue canton represents the freedom that would shine forth in the so-called "Dark Continent." The canton itself represents Africa. The 11 stripes are said to stand, in this case, for the signatories of Liberia's Declaration of Independence.

All the counties of Liberia have local flags, but the extent of their use is unclear.

THE PRESIDENT'S FLAG
There is also a flag for the President, using a shield in the form of the national flag. Whether this is actually in use is doubtful, in view of the civil war in Liberia since 1990.

THE PRESIDENT'S FLAG

Shield is derived from features of the national flag

Four stars representing the Supreme Commander

IVORY COAST

Ratio: *2:3* Adopted: *December 3, 1959* Usage: *National and Civil*

Orange represents the savanna grasslands

Green recalls the coastal forests

The design is modeled on the French Tricolore

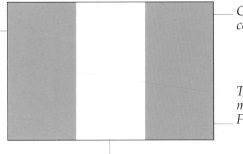

White represents the country's rivers

AFRICA

THE IVORY COAST (Côte d'Ivoire) was originally part of French West Africa. It became independent in its own right on August 7, 1960.

After independence, the Ivory Coast formed a loose alliance of West African states. The flags of these states were influenced both by the Pan-African colors first used by Ghana, and also by the model of the French *Tricolore*, the flag of the former colonial power.

ALLIANCE OF WEST AFRICAN STATES
The colors chosen for the Ivory Coast's flag were also used by Niger, with which Ivory Coast had an alliance (the resemblance to the colors of Ireland is coincidental). They were intended to symbolize the following: orange represents the savanna grasslands, white the rivers, and green the coastal forests.

Another interpretation is that they symbolize progress, hope, and national unity. The flag was adopted in 1959, just prior to independence.

THE NATIONAL ARMS
The coat of arms, which has a green shield charged with an elephant's head, is based on the emblem of the *Rassemblement Démocratique Africaine*, the dominant political party at the time of independence. Originally the elephant's head was on a blue shield, but this was altered in 1964 to green, to match the national flag. The shield is supported by two palm trees. Behind is a rising sun. On a scroll at the base of the arms is the title of the state, *Republique de Côte d'Ivoire*.

BURKINA

Ratio: 2:3   Adopted: *August 4, 1984*   Usage: *National and Civil*

Red recalls the 1984 revolution

The star is the guiding light of the revolution

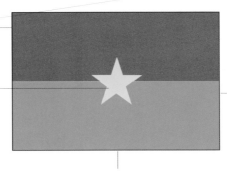

Red, yellow, and green are Pan-African colors

Green represents Burkina's abundant natural resources

AFRICA

BURKINA, originally known as Upper Volta, was once a French colony. It became self-governing in 1958 and fully independent in 1960.

The original flag of Upper Volta, adopted at independence, contained three horizontal stripes of black, white, and red. These simple colors represented the three major tributaries of the River Volta, which flow south through the country.

A NEW NATIONAL FLAG

In August 1984 there was a coup, and a new flag and emblem were adopted. The new flag is in the Pan-African colors, reflecting both a break with the country's colonial past and its unity with other African ex-colonies. The red is also said to symbolize the revolution and the green the abundance of natural riches. The yellow star placed over the red and green stripes is the guiding light of the revolution.

THE NATIONAL ARMS

The coat of arms, which was adopted in September 1997, shows a shield in the colors of the national flag. The arms are held by two horses, which represent the nobility of the people. Two crossed lances show the will of the people to defend their country, and an open book and two ears of millet symbolize their will to educate and feed themselves. At the top of the arms is a scroll, inscribed with the name Burkina – the country of the upright people. At the base, another scroll carries the national motto: Unity, Development, Justice.

GHANA

Ratio: 2:3   Adopted: *March 6, 1957*   Usage: *National*

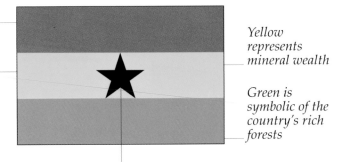

Red recalls the blood shed by freedom fighters

Ghana was the first country to use the Pan-African colors of red, yellow, green and black

Yellow represents mineral wealth

Green is symbolic of the country's rich forests

The star of African freedom

AFRICA

PREVIOUSLY the Gold Coast, Ghana became independent from Britain in 1957. It took its new name from that of an historic African empire.

Kwame Nkrumah, Ghana's first leader after independence, was the first to introduce the politically symbolic Pan-African colors – red, yellow, green, and black – into African flags. They were ultimately derived from the 19th-century Ethiopian colors and have now become associated with the Rastafarian movement in the West Indies. The flag also became the inspiration for numerous other African flags during the period of decolonization.

Ghana followed the flag patterns established in the United Kingdom, and so has a both a red ensign for use on civil vessels and a white ensign for naval vessels. This use of several flags sets it apart from other West African states, which normally have only one all-purpose flag.

GHANAIAN RED ENSIGN

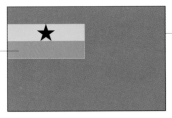

The national flag is placed in the canton

The field is in the style of the British Red Ensign

TOGO

Ratio: 2:3   Adopted: *April 27, 1960*   Usage: *National and Civil*

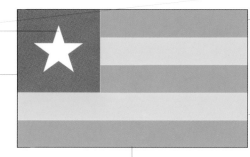

The star of hope

Red symbolizes
the blood shed
during the
struggle for
independence

Green
represents
agricultural
wealth

Yellow reflects
Togo's mineral
wealth

*The five stripes represent the
five regions of Togo*

AFRICA

TOGO, once a German colony, was divided
between France and Britain in 1914. The French
part became independent, as Togo, in 1960.

During the period of autonomy from
1956–1960, the flag was green with
two yellow stars arranged
diagonally with the French *Tricolore*
in the canton.

On independence in 1960, the
present flag was adopted. The five
stripes stand for the regions of Togo,
and are in green and yellow to
signify its agricultural and mineral
resources. The red canton is for the
blood of those who struggled for
independence, while the white star is
for hope, as on Liberia's flag.

The national emblem contains two
lions holding bows and arrows, and
a sun with the country's initials.
Above the sun is the national motto.

EMBLEM OF TOGO

The national motto,
Union, Paix,
Solidarité, *meaning*
"Unity, Peace,
Solidarity"

RT stands for the title
of the state République
Togolaise

Two lions are shown
carrying bows and
arrows to protect the
homeland

BENIN

Ratio: *2:3*   Adopted: *November 16, 1959*   Usage: *National and Civil*

Red, yellow, and green are Pan-African colors

The colors symbolize African unity and nationalism

AFRICA

ORIGINALLY KNOWN as Dahomey, Benin became autonomous in 1958 and independent from France in 1960. Its name was changed in 1975.

The flag used today is the same as that adopted in 1959, although after the revolution of December 1975, a green flag with a red star in the canton was used. The original flag was restored in 1990, as was the original national emblem. The new name of the country was retained.

Benin has both a seal and a coat of arms. The seal depicts a *pirogue,* or African canoe, with a bow and arrow, and two clubs. The arms consists of a quartered shield depicting a local Somba fortress, the medal of the Order of the Star of Benin, a palm tree, and a sailing ship. The motto is *Fraternité, Justice, Travail* meaning "Fraternity, Justice, Work."

ARMS OF BENIN

The Horns of Plenty spilling out ears of corn are symbolic of riches from the land

The Order of Star of Benin

A Somba fortress

The national motto, meaning "Fraternity, Justice, Work"

NIGERIA

Ratio: *1:2*   Adopted: *October 1, 1960*   Usage: *National*

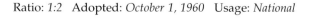

White symbolizes peace and unity

Green represents the land

AFRICA

NIGERIA WAS FORMED in 1914 from several British colonies and protectorates. In 1954 it became a federation and in 1960 achieved independence.

The national flag is an adaptation of the winning entry in a competition held in 1959. The original had a red sun with streaming rays placed at the top of the white stripe. This was removed by the judges and the flag has not been altered since.

Like Ghana, Nigeria has special flags for civil and naval vessels and at one time the states also had flags.

The coat of arms was granted in 1960, but the motto has been altered since then to include the words "Peace and Progress." The shield represents the confluence of two rivers, and the crest is a red eagle. It all stands on a green base strewn with the *Costus spectabilis* flower.

ARMS OF NIGERIA

The red eagle symbolizing strength is the national badge

The Costus spectabilis *is the national flower*

The confluence of the Niger and Benuë rivers

The two white horses symbolize dignity

The national motto – "Unity and Faith, Peace and Progress"

UNITY AND FAITH, PEACE AND PROGRESS

CAMEROON

Ratio: 2:3   Adopted: *May 20, 1975*   Usage: *National and Civil*

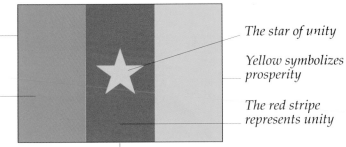

The pattern of the flag reflects the French Tricolore

Green represents hope

The star of unity

Yellow symbolizes prosperity

The red stripe represents unity

Red, yellow, and green are the Pan-African colors

AFRICA

CAMEROON WAS originally a German colony, which was partitioned by the French and the British after World War I.

The French area became autonomous on January 1, 1959 and independent a year later. A national flag was adopted during the period of French control and was the first West African flag after that of Ghana to use the red, yellow, and green colors. The actual design is based on the French *Tricolore*. The original design of 1959 did not have a star.

A NEW UNITED FLAG

In 1961, the southern part of British Cameroon joined the former French colony to form the current state of Cameroon. To mark this, two yellow stars were placed in the upper hoist. In 1975, the two stars were replaced by a single star in the center of the flag to symbolize the new unity of the state.

THE NATIONAL ARMS

The coat of arms, like the flag, has been altered to reflect the changes in the constitution. The date on the original upper scroll reflected the date of independence of French Cameroon. This has now been removed, leaving just the name of the state on the scroll; there is now only one yellow star in the green on the shield. The main features of the current arms are a map of the country, a balance, and two crossed fasces or local axes. The shield is divided in the colors of the national flag: green, red, and yellow.

EQUATORIAL GUINEA

Ratio: 2:3   Adopted: *October 12, 1968*   Usage: *National and Civil*

The blue triangle represents the sea

White stands for peace

Green reflects the country's agricultural lands

The national arms have always appeared on the flag

Red symbolizes the country's independence

AFRICA

Cameroon
EQUATORIAL GUINEA
Congo
Gabon

EQUATORIAL GUINEA includes the former Spanish colonies of Río Muni, the island of Fernando Po (Bioko), and other islands in the Gulf of Guinea.

The flag was first flown on the day of independence, October 12, 1968, and it showed the national emblem in the center. However, in 1972, during the regime of Francisco Nguema, a different national emblem appeared on the flag. The original coat of arms was restored after Nguema was deposed in August 1979.

ARMS OF EQUATORIAL GUINEA
The arms consists of a silver shield charged with a silk-cotton tree, which was derived from the arms of Río Muni. Above the shield is an arc of six, six-pointed stars, that represent Río Muni and the offshore islands. Beneath the shield is a scroll with the national motto.

ARMS OF EQUATORIAL GUINEA

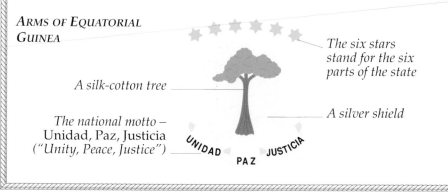

The six stars stand for the six parts of the state

A silk-cotton tree

A silver shield

The national motto – Unidad, Paz, Justicia ("Unity, Peace, Justice")

UNIDAD PAZ JUSTICIA

SAO TOME & PRINCIPE

Ratio: *1:2*   Adopted: *November 5, 1975*   Usage: *National and Civil*

The red triangle recalls the struggle for independence, as on the flags of Ghana and Togo

Green, red, yellow, and black are Pan-African colors

The two stars stand for the two islands

AFRICA

Príncipe   Equatorial Guinea
SAO TOME & PRINCIPE
São Tomé   Gabon

SAO TOME AND PRINCIPE are a pair of islands in the Gulf of Guinea that formerly belonged to Portugal. They became independent in 1975.

The flag is based on the party flag of the Movement for the Liberation of Sao Tome and Principe (MLSTP). It was retained even after the party lost its monopoly of power in 1990.

The combination of red, yellow, and green with black stars, is based on the flag of Ghana, with the stars standing for the two islands.

The shield within the national arms is in the form of a cocoa pod, on which is depicted a cocoa palm, the country's main export. Above this is a star representing freedom. The supporters are two pigeons standing on a scroll with the national motto – *Unidade, Disciplina, Trabajo* ("Unity, Discipline, Work").

ARMS OF SAO TOME AND PRINCIPE

The crest, a blue star, stands for African freedom

The shield is in the form of a cocoa pod

The upper scroll bears the title of the state

The national motto – Unidade, Disciplina, Trabajo ("Unity, Discipline, Work")

GABON

Ratio: *3:4*   Adopted: *August 9, 1960*   Usage: *National and Civil*

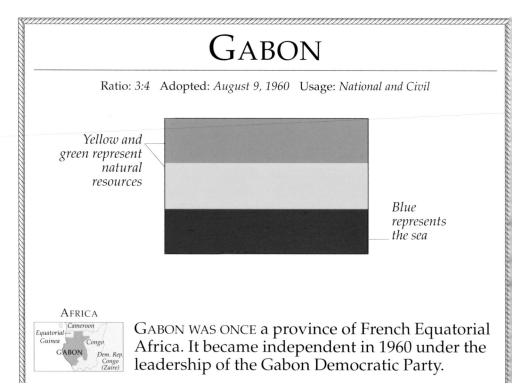

Yellow and green represent natural resources

Blue represents the sea

AFRICA

GABON WAS ONCE a province of French Equatorial Africa. It became independent in 1960 under the leadership of the Gabon Democratic Party.

The original flag was adopted in 1959 and was similar to the present one, but with stripes of unequal width and the French *Tricolore* in the canton. The *Tricolore* was dropped at independence and the thin yellow stripe, symbolizing the Equator, was enlarged. Now the colors represent the sun, the sea, and the country's natural resources, particularly timber.

The coat of arms is of European style and is in the colors of the flag. The shield is supported by two black panthers and an *okoumé* tree, symbolic of the timber trade. The coat of arms is unusual in having a Latin motto – *Uniti Progrediamur*, beneath the branches of the tree.

ARMS OF GABON

A Latin motto – Unite Progrediamur *"We go forward in Unity"*

A second motto means *"Union, Work, Justice"*

The okoumé *tree is symbolic of the timber trade*

Two black panthers support the shield

The ship represents Gabon moving toward a brighter future

CONGO

Ratio: *2:3*   Adopted: *November 20, 1959*   Usage: *National and Civil*

The Pan-African colors of red, yellow, and green

The distinctive diagonal pattern sets it apart from other Pan-African flags

AFRICA

CONGO WAS A French colony until independence as Congo-Brazzaville in 1960. After a coup in 1964, it became the People's Republic (1970–91).

The current flag was originally adopted for the autonomous republic, established on August 18, 1959. It is in the Pan-African colors used by many other West African flags. It was retained without change when full independence was achieved in 1960.

THE PEOPLE'S REPUBLIC 1970–91
Following the Marxist revolution in 1964, no new national flag was officially adopted until the People's Republic was formed in 1970. This flag was red and contained the national emblem in the canton. The emblem depicted a wreath containing a crossed hoe and hammer, and a gold star. This represented the Communist regime which had taken power.

AN OLD FLAG FOR A NEW ERA
At the National Conference for the restoration of democracy in 1991, which restored a multiparty democracy, the original flag, arms, and national anthem were all reinstated. This decision was made official on June 4, 1991.

ARMS OF CONGO
The coat of arms was originally adopted in 1963 and was designed by the European heraldist Louis Mühlemann, who also designed the arms of Gabon. It follows a traditional European heraldic style.

ANGOLA

Ratio: *2:3*   Adopted: *November 11, 1975*   Usage: *National and Civil*

The cogwheel and machete are emblems of agriculture and of industry

The design is based on flag of the MPLA

The emblems are similar to the Soviet-style hammer and sickle

ORIGINALLY A PORTUGUESE COLONY, Angola was eventually liberated by the People's Liberation Movement of Angola in 1975.

The flag of the People's Liberation Movement of Angola (MPLA) is like the present national flag but with a yellow star. The half cogwheel and machete on the national flag were added to create an emblem reminiscent of the hammer and sickle on the Soviet flag.

The national arms also features the cogwheel, star, and machete, but includes a hoe. These symbols are placed on a background that, like the emblem on the flag, is similar to the devices used in Soviet designs. The cogwheel is balanced by a wreath of cotton, coffee, and corn, and an open book. On the scroll is "Republic of Angola," the state name.

ARMS OF ANGOLA

These are emblems of agriculture and of industry

The book is symbolic of the importance of education

The Soviet-style emblem is still in use

The state name, in Portuguese – República de Angola – is placed on the scroll

ZAMBIA

Ratio: *2:3*   Adopted: *October 24, 1964*   Usage: *National and Civil*

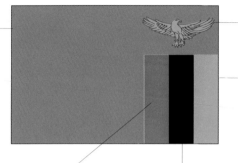

The green field represents Zambia's agriculture

The eagle is taken from the national arms

Yellow represents the country's copper

Red recalls the struggle for independence

Black stands for the people

AFRICA

ZAMBIA WAS FORMERLY the British colony of Northern Rhodesia. It was granted full independence in 1964.

Although the United Nationalist Independence Party is no longer dominant in Zambia, the party's colors remain in the bottom left of the flag, designed by graphic artists just prior to independence. The eagle is taken from the national coat of arms, which is based on those of the former Northern Rhodesia.

In the arms, the eagle that once appeared in the upper part of the shield, forms the crest, above a crossed pickax and hoe. White and black bars on the shield represent the famous Victoria Falls. The supporters are an African man and woman and the motto on the base reads "One Zambia, One Nation."

ARMS OF ZAMBIA

The eagle of liberty

The pickax and hoe are emblems of agriculture and industry

The shield stands on an allegorical landscape

The shield represents the white waters of the River Zambezi flowing over black rock at the Victoria Falls

TANZANIA

Ratio: 2:3   Adopted: *June 30, 1964*   Usage: *National and Civil*

Green and black, taken from the old Tanganyikan flag, represent the land and the people

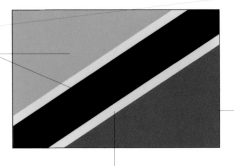

Blue, taken from the flag of Zanzibar, represents the sea

Yellow symbolizes mineral wealth

TANGANYIKA BECAME INDEPENDENT from Britain in 1961 and in 1964, it merged with the Republic of Zanzibar to form Tanzania.

The original flag of independent Tanganyika was derived from that of the Tanganyika African National Union, the dominant party at the time. This had horizontal stripes of green-black-green. For the national flag, yellow fimbriations were placed between the green and the black.

Derived from the Afro-Shirazi Party, the flag of Zanzibar is green, black, and blue stripes, with a vertical white stripe along the hoist.

A NEW UNITED FLAG

When the two countries united to form Tanzania, a new national flag was created that combined the colors of Tanganyika and Zanzibar. The country's coat of arms was also altered to include the new national flag in the shield, again to reflect the new union of the two countries.

FLAG OF ZANZIBAR

Blue was incorporated in the new national flag of Tanzania

A white fimbriation runs along the hoist

These are the colors of the Afro-Shirazi Party, who overthrew the ruling Sultan in 1964

MALAWI

Ratio: 2:3   Adopted: *July 6, 1964*   Usage: *National and Civil*

Black is symbolic of Malawi's African heritage

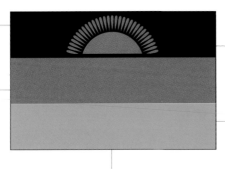

The rising sun symbolizes a new dawn

Red represents the blood shed for freedom

Green represents the land

These are the colors of the Malawi Congress Party

AFRICA

As NYASALAND, Malawi formed part of British Rhodesia and Nyasaland from 1953–63. It became fully independent in 1964.

The colors of the flag are the same as those of Malawi Congress Party (MCP) which led the country to independence in 1964. The MCP flag was derived from the flag popularized by Marcus Garvey (*see page 7*) at the time of the World War I, as the flag of Africa or "Ethiopia," symbolizing an African renaissance. On Malawi's national flag the rising sun or *kwacha* was added in red. The *kwacha* also appeared on the colonial coat of arms adopted in 1914. It was retained on the current arms granted with the flag in 1964.

THE PRESIDENT'S FLAG

The flag of the President has a bright red field. It uses the lion passant found in the center of the coat of arms, with the name "Malawi."

THE PRESIDENT'S FLAG

The name of the state

The lion passant is taken from the coat of arms

ZIMBABWE

Ratio: *1:2*   Adopted: *April 18, 1980*   Usage: *National and Civil*

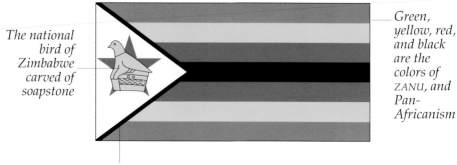

The national bird of Zimbabwe carved of soapstone

Green, yellow, red, and black are the colors of ZANU, *and* Pan-Africanism

Black represents the new leaders, and white, their desire for peace

AFRICA

Zambia
ZIMBABWE
Mozambique
Botswana
South Africa

ZIMBABWE, the name of an ancient African city, is now applied to the whole country, which was formerly known as Rhodesia.

The Zimbabwe African National Union (ZANU) led the struggle for self-determination in the 1970s, and its flag was used as the basis for the new national flag. The ZANU flag is composed of concentric panels of green, yellow, red, with a central black panel – the colors of pan-Africanism. The national flag has these colors simply arranged in stripes. Toward the hoist is a white triangle with a black edge, symbolizing the new leaders and their desire for peace. Within this is the bird of Zimbabwe on a red star.

THE ZIMBABWE BIRD
The bird is representative of those found in the ruins of the ancient city of Zimbabwe and has been a local symbol since 1924. The star stands for an international outlook.

EMBLEM OF ZIMBABWE

The star represents the country's international outlook

A representation of the ancient city of Zimbabwe

The soapstone bird is the national emblem

MOZAMBIQUE

Ratio: *2:3*   Adopted: *May 1, 1983*   Usage: *National and Civil*

Green symbolizes
the riches of
the land

Black represents
the African
continent

Red represents
the struggle for
independence

The white
fimbriations
signify peace

Yellow symbolizes the
country's minerals

Malawi
Zambia   Tanzania
Zimbabwe   MOZAMBIQUE
South   Madagascar
Africa

MOZAMBIQUE WAS A Portuguese colony before becoming independent under the single-party rule of FRELIMO in 1975.

The original flag of the *Frente da Libertação da Moçambique* (FRELIMO), the leading political party in Mozambique, also had green, black, and yellow horizontal stripes separated by white fimbriations. In the hoist was a red triangle. The black, green, and yellow were derived from the flag of the African National Congress, used in South Africa. On independence the colors were rearranged to form the national flag, in rays emanating from the upper hoist. Over this was a white cogwheel containing the hoe, rifle, book, and star that appear on the present flag. The flag was altered in 1983; the colors were arranged in horizontal stripes, and the star of Marxism was made larger. It is likely that a new, nonpartisan flag will be introduced.

EMBLEM OF MOZAMBIQUE

The hoe represents the
country's agriculture

The star symbolizes
Marxism and
internationalism

The rifle stands for
defense and vigilance

The open book
symbolizes the
importance of education

101

NAMIBIA

Ratio: *2:3*   Adopted: *March 21, 1990*   Usage: *National and Civil*

The sun is the emblem of life and energy

Red, white, and blue were the colors of the Democratic Turnhalle Alliance

Blue, red, and green were the colors of SWAPO

AFRICA

NAMIBIA, once German South West Africa, passed into South African control after the World War I, until gaining independence in 1990.

The national flag combines the colors of the South West African People's Organization (SWAPO), which liberated Namibia in 1990, and those of the Democratic Turnhalle Alliance, another Namibian political party. The gold sun, which is similar to that on the flag of Taiwan, represents life and energy.

ARMS OF NAMIBIA

The coat of arms, adopted with the flag, appears on the President's Flag. The shield is of the same pattern as the national flag and is supported by a pair of oryx. On a sand dune beneath is a *welwitschia* plant, found in the Namib Desert. The crest is a fish eagle on a chieftain's crown.

ARMS OF NAMIBIA

The shield is based on the national flag

The welwitschia plant is found in the Namib Desert

The fish eagle stands on a chieftain's crown

Two oryx support the shield

The national motto – "Unity, Liberty, Justice"

BOTSWANA

Ratio: 2:3   Adopted: *September 30, 1966*   Usage: *National and Civil*

Black and white symbolize the harmony of the people

Blue represents both water and life

AFRICA

BOTSWANA, originally known as British Bechuanaland, is now known by its Setswana name. Independence was achieved in 1966.

Unusual for Africa, the national flag of Botswana is not derived from that of the dominant political party. Neither does it use the Pan-African colors.

PULA – LIFE-GIVING RAIN
Instead, it is based on the idea of life-giving rain, an essential element in the drought-prone country. This is also reflected in the Setswana word *pula*, which forms the national motto. This means not only "water" and "rain" but also the life that is derived from it.

The two horizontal blue stripes represent rain and water. The importance of water is also a feature on the flag of Lesotho. The black stripe fimbriated with white in the center of the flag represents the African and European populations of Botswana living in harmony and the national animal, the zebra.

ARMS OF BOTSWANA
The coat of arms that appears on the President's Flag was adopted in 1966. The African shield depicts three cogwheels and a bull's head separated by three wavy bars of water. The supporters are two zebras, holding an elephant tusk and a sorghum plant, the country's staple crop. Some also interpret the zebras, with their black and white stripes, as being symbolic of racial integration.

LESOTHO

Ratio: 2:3   Adopted: *January 20, 1987*   Usage: *National and Civil*

A simplified
version of the
arms showing a
shield, a spear,
and a local club

White
represents
peace

Green
signifies
plenty

Blue is symbolic of the importance
of water and rain

AFRICA

LESOTHO WAS FORMERLY known as British Basutoland but is now known by its Sesotho name. It became independent in 1966.

The flag hoisted on the day of independence was based on the colors of the then dominant Basuto National Party and depicted a typical African straw hat.

THE NEW NATIONAL FLAG
Following a *coup d'etat* in 1986, the original flag was discarded and the present flag adopted on January 20, 1987. Unlike its predecessor, it does not contain any political colors, but instead is intended to represent the words of the national motto: *Khotso-Pula-Nala*, meaning "Peace, Rain, Plenty," by the colors white, blue, and green. Water is also symbolized on the national flag of Botswana. In the canton is a simplified

version of part of the coat of arms which was adopted on independence in 1966.

ROYAL ARMS OF LESOTHO
On the national flag only the outline of the shield is shown, with its tufted spine, and two weapons, but on the Royal Standard the whole coat of arms appears in color.

The shield, of African design, contains a crocodile, which is a symbol of King Moshoeshoe I, who founded the state in 1824. It stands on a representation of Mount Thaba Bosiu, the Mountain of Night, and is supported by two Basuto ponies. Behind the shield is a spear and a *knobkerrie*, a local club.

SWAZILAND

Ratio: *2:3*   Adopted: *October 30, 1967*   Usage: *National and Civil*

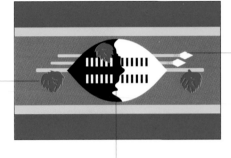

Injobo *tassles,
made from
widowbird and
loury feathers*

Assegais *are
Swazi spears*

*The pattern of the shield is taken from
the Emasotsha Regiment*

AFRICA

SWAZILAND was a British Protectorate until 1968.
It is now ruled by the Swazi royal family who
founded the kingdom in the 19th century.

The flag is based on one given by the late King Sobhuza II to the Swazi Pioneer Corps in 1941. On it is an Emasotsha shield, laid horizontally. The shield is reinforced by a staff from which hang *injobo* tassles – bunches of feathers of the widowbird and the loury. They also decorate the shield. Above the staff are two *assegais* – local spears. The shield and *assegais* appear on the national arms, which is supported by a lion and an elephant, symbolic of the King and of the Queen Mother. The crest is an otter-skin headdress decorated with widowbird feathers, and the motto is *Siyinqaba* meaning "We are the fortress."

ARMS OF SWAZILAND

*A lion, symbolic
of the King*

*The national
motto – "We are
the fortress"*

*A headdress and
widowbird feathers*

*An elephant,
symbolic of the
Queen Mother*

SOUTH AFRICA

Ratio: *2:3* Adopted: *April 27, 1994* Usage: *National and Civil*

The overall design conveys convergence and unification

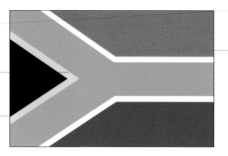

Red, white, and blue are taken from the colors of the Boer republics

Yellow, black, and green are taken from the ANC flag

AFRICA

THE UNION OF SOUTH AFRICA was formed in 1910 and the republic in 1961. In 1994 a democratic, multiracial constitution was adopted.

South Africa had no distinctive flag until 1928 when a national flag was adopted based on the orange, white, and blue tricolor used by the first Dutch settlers, with three smaller flags in the center for Britain, the Transvaal, and the Orange Free State.

When a multiracial democracy came into prospect, attempts were made to find a new flag, and the present design, created by the Chief Herald of South Africa, was adopted.

A NEW FLAG FOR A NEW ERA
The new South African flag combines the colors of the Boer republics with those of the African National Congress (ANC), whose flag was adopted in 1917. The Y-shape represents the convergence of old traditions with new and the progress of the united state into the future.

AFRICAN NATIONAL CONGRESS FLAG

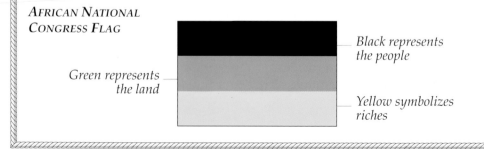

Black represents the people

Green represents the land

Yellow symbolizes riches

SEYCHELLES

Ratio: *1:2*   Adopted: *January 8, 1996*   Usage: *National and Civil*

The flag now includes blue and yellow, the colors of the Democratic Party

Red, white, and green are the colors of the SPUP

AFRICA

THE SEYCHELLES became independent from France in 1976. In 1977, a *coup d'état* brought the Seychelles Peoples United Party to power.

The Seychelles has had three flags since independence. After the coup of 1977 a new national flag based on the party flag of the ruling SPUP was adopted. This used their colors of red, white, and green.

Following the adoption of the Constitution of 1993, the existence of other parties was permitted and the latest flag allows for the colors of the Democratic Party to be included in a striking new design.

The coat of arms was adopted in 1976 and it has been only slightly altered since then. It is based on the old colonial badge and depicts the most famous inhabitant of the islands, the giant tortoise.

ARMS OF THE SEYCHELLES

Two sailfish support the arms

The giant tortoise and palm have been in use in the arms since the 19th century

The crest is a paille-en-queue, *a native bird of the Seychelles*

A Latin motto – Finis Coronat Opus, *meaning "The end crowns the work," was chosen in the 19th century*

COMOROS

Ratio: 3:5   Adopted: *January 2002*   Usage: *Government and Civil*

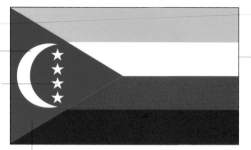

The crescent of Islam

Four stars represent the four islands of the Comoros

Each stripe represents one of the four islands

Green is the traditional color of Islam

THE COMOROS became independent in 1975, although the island of Mayotte did not join the new state and remains a French dependency.

The present flag is based on one adopted at independence, which included stars for the four main islands (including Mayotte) and a crescent to symbolize Islam. The original flag was mainly red, to underline the socialist aspirations of the country. This was dropped in 1978 in favor of a green flag, with the crescent and stars in white.

The Constitution of 1996 established the present form, which also includes the monograms of Allah and of Muhammad in the corners.

Comoros adopted a new name, constitution and flag in January 2002. The four stars, the crescent moon, and the green of Islam have been moved into a triangle. Each stripe of yellow, white, red, and blue represents one of the four islands.

THE NATIONAL FLAG
1996–2002

A monogram of Allah

A monogram of the Prophet Muhammad

MADAGASCAR

Ratio: *2:3*   Adopted: *October 14, 1958*   Usage: *National and Civil*

Red and white were the colors of the Kingdom of Madagascar

Green represents the Hova, the former peasant class

AFRICA

MADAGASCAR

MADAGASCAR was annexed by France in 1895, and the monarchy abolished two years later. It achieved independence in 1960.

The flag was introduced when self-government was achieved in 1958 and was retained on independence. The red and white are said to symbolize the earlier Merina Kingdom, whose flags were all red and white, with the addition of green for the Hova, the former peasant class. The coat of arms has changed several times since independence. That of the present republic, introduced in March 1993, shows a map of the island with a spray of leaves. Beneath these is a paddy field surmounted by the head of a zebu. The motto reads "Fatherland, Liberty, Justice." Above the design is the country name.

ARMS OF MADAGASCAR

The state title is in Malagasy, the local language

The national motto – "Fatherland, Liberty, Justice"

The leaves of the traveler's tree

An outline of Madagascar

A stylized paddy field and a zebu, a local ox

MAURITIUS

Ratio: *2:3*   Adopted: *January 9, 1968*   Usage: *National*

Red reflects
independence

Blue for the
color of the
Indian Ocean

Yellow symbolizes
a bright future

Green represents the lush
vegetation of the island

AFRICA

MAURITIUS WAS TAKEN over by Britain from France in 1810. The colony achieved independence in 1968 and became a republic in 1992.

The flag was designed by the College of Arms in Britain prior to independence and is a simple statement of the colors found in the coat of arms.

ARMS OF MAURITIUS
The coat of arms was granted on August 25, 1906, and depicts various attributes of the island. In the lower right quarter is a key and on the left-hand side is a white star, which are referred to in the Latin motto, *Stella Clavisque Maris Indici* ("The star and the key of the Indian Ocean"). The supporters are a dodo and a deer each holding a sugar cane, the island's staple crop.

ARMS OF MAURITIUS

A dodo, extinct since
the 18th century

A ship symbolizing
colonization

The star and key
are referred to
in the motto

Palm trees represent
the country's tropical
vegetation

A deer

The national motto –
"The star and the key
of the Indian Ocean"

STELLA CLAVISQUE MARIS INDICI

110

ICELAND

Ratio: *18:25*   Adopted: *June 19, 1915*   Usage: *National and Civil*

White recalls
the ice and snow
that covers
Iceland

Deep blue
represents
the
Atlantic
Ocean

Red represents the fire produced
by the island's volcanoes

EUROPE

Greenland   ICELAND

RULED BY THE DANES from the 14th century,
Iceland became a realm within the kingdom of
Denmark in 1918, and a republic in 1944.

Iceland's first national flag was a white cross on a deep blue background. It was first paraded in 1897. The modern flag dates from 1915, when a red cross was inserted into the white cross of the original flag. It was adopted in 1918 and became the national flag when Iceland gained independence from Denmark in 1944.

FIRE, ICE, AND WATER
For the Icelandic people the flag's coloring represents a vision of their country's landscape. The colors stand for three of the elements that make up the island: fire, ice, and water.

The President's flag is a swallow-tailed flag with the national arms in the center. It was adopted in 1944.

THE PRESIDENT'S FLAG

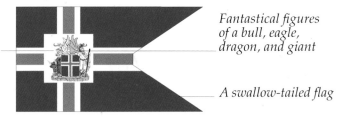

According to legend,
the figures on the
shield are guardian
spirits who defend
the island from
attack

Fantastical figures
of a bull, eagle,
dragon, and giant

A swallow-tailed flag

NORWAY

Ratio: *8:11*   Adopted: *July 17, 1821*   Usage: *National and Civil*

The red, white, and blue colors were influenced by the French Tricolore — a symbol of liberty — and by the flags of the US and UK

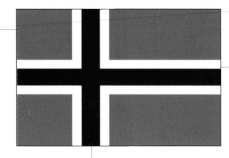

Off-centered white cross on a red field is taken from the Danish flag

The blue cross of Sweden

RULED BY DENMARK from 1397, Norway passed to Sweden in 1814. It gained independence in 1905, when its union with Sweden was dissolved.

Until 1814, the Norwegian flag bore the Danish red and white cross. The current flag was born in 1821, during the period when Norway was united with Sweden. The flag combines these two influences; its red and white coloring was taken from the Danish flag, and a blue cross was added overall. These three colors were chosen in honor of the French

Tricolore, a symbol of revolution and liberty. They were also the colors of the flags of the United States of America and the United Kingdom, two other countries that were not ruled by an absolute monarch.

The Royal Standard consists of a banner of the Royal Arms, dating back to the Middle Ages. It depicts a lion rampant on a red field.

THE ROYAL STANDARD

The standard dates back to the Middle Ages

A tall, slender lion bearing the ax of St. Olav

DENMARK

Ratio: *28:37*   Adopted: *1625*   Usage: *National and Civil*

The off-centered cross is the basis for other Scandinavian countries' flags

According to legend, a red flag with a white cross appeared as a sign from heaven

EUROPE

DENMARK IS EUROPE'S oldest kingdom, dating back to the 10th century. The present queen rules under a constitution granted in 1953.

Besides being the oldest monarchy in Europe, Denmark also has the oldest flag, known as the *Dannebrog*, or Danish cloth. Legend says that a blood-red flag with a white cross appeared as a sign from heaven to King Valdemar II during the conquest of Estonia in 1219. In reality, the flag may have been a gift from the pope during the Crusades.

THE SCANDINAVIAN CROSS
The flag was originally square, but its design was elongated, and the arm of the cross in the fly was extended. It has become a model for other flags.

Overseas Territories

FAEROE ISLANDS

The Faeroe Islands are a self-governing territory of Denmark. The flag has the Norwegian colors in a new arrangement. This recalls that they were once part of Norway.

GREENLAND

Greenland's flag was designed by a local artist and adopted in 1985. In the Danish colors, white represents the ice that covers most of the island, and red is for the Sun.

SWEDEN

Ratio: *5:8*   Adopted: *June 22, 1906*   Usage: *National and Civil*

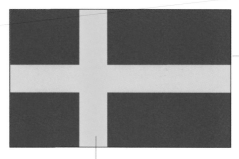

The yellow and blue colors are taken from the national arms

The distinctive Scandinavian cross is taken from the flag of Denmark

EUROPE

UNTIL 1523, when King Gustav Vasa laid the foundation of Sweden as a separate state, the country was under the influence of Denmark.

The present flag was adopted in 1906, but it was first used in a similar form almost four centuries before. The design is based on the Scandinavian cross. The flag's blue and yellow colors are thought to come from the national coat of arms – three gold crowns in a blue field – which originated in the 14th century. A national flag day is celebrated each year on June 6. On this day in 1523 King Gustav Vasa was elected; on the same date in 1809, Sweden adopted a new constitution.

SWEDISH ROYAL STANDARD
The coat of arms is placed in the center of the Royal Standard, which is used on special occasions by Parliament and dates from the 1440s.

THE ROYAL STANDARD

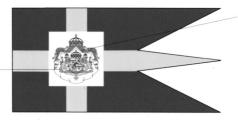

The shield is supported by two golden lions

The triple crown symbolizes the Three Wise Men, a Swedish emblem since 1336

FINLAND

Ratio: *11:18*   Adopted: *May 29, 1918*   Usage: *National and Civil*

Blue represents
Finland's blue
skies and its
thousands of
lakes

The overall
design is
based on the
Scandinavian
cross

White recalls the snows of winter

EUROPE

FINLAND WAS PART OF Sweden from the 12th century. From 1809 until independence in 1917, it was part of the Russian Empire.

Like Sweden's, Finland's national flag is based on the Scandinavian cross. It was adopted after independence from Russia, when many patriotic Finns wanted a special flag for their country, but its design dates back to the 19th century. The blue coloring is said to represent the country's thousands of lakes and the sky, with white for the snow that covers the land in winter. This color combination has also been used over the centuries in various Finnish provincial, military, and town flags.

THE ÅLAND ISLANDS

The Åland Islands are an autonomous group of Finnish islands with their own flag since 1954. The design incorporates a Scandinavian cross.

THE FLAG OF THE
ÅLAND ISLANDS

Red and yellow
are taken from
the arms of
Finland

Blue and yellow
represent Sweden; the
islands have a large
Swedish population

ESTONIA

Ratio: *7:11*   Adopted: *May 8, 1990*   Usage: *National and Civil*

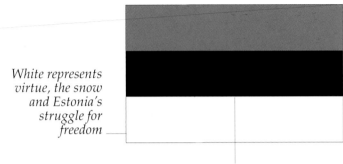

Blue represents loyalty and Estonia's sky, sea, and lakes

White represents virtue, the snow and Estonia's struggle for freedom

Black is symbolic of past oppression and the soil

EUROPE

AFTER WORLD WAR II, Estonia became a republic within the Soviet Union. It gained independence from the Soviet Union in 1991.

The tricolor was first adopted by students in 1881 during uprisings against occupying Russian Tsarist forces. It was readopted as the national flag in 1990 just prior to independence. The colors represent Estonian history, folk costumes, and landscape. Blue is the color of loyalty and also represents the sky, sea, and lakes. Black symbolizes the past suffering of the people, the soil, and the traditional black peasant's jacket. White represents virtue and the struggle for freedom. It is also the color of birch bark and snow.

The great coat of arms was originally the emblem of a 13th-century Danish king.

GREAT ARMS OF ESTONIA

The shield is surrounded by golden branches of oak

Three blue leopards are ranged on a gold shield

LATVIA

Ratio: *1:2*   Adopted: *February 27, 1990*   Usage: *National and Civil*

White may
stand for the
sheet used to
wrap the
wounded
Latvian
leader

Red
recalls the
blood shed
by the
wounded
leader

Red also represents Latvians'
willingness to defend their liberty

EUROPE

OVER THE CENTURIES, Latvia has been invaded by Swedes, Poles, and Russians. It became independent from the Soviet Union in 1991.

Though officially adopted in 1922, the Latvian flag was in use as early as the 13th century, but its use was suppressed during Soviet rule.

The red color is sometimes described as symbolizing the readiness of the Latvians to give the blood from their hearts for freedom. An alternative interpretation,

according to one legend, is that a Latvian leader was wounded in battle, and the edges of the white sheet in which he was wrapped were stained by his blood.

The coat of arms depicts a tripartite shield recalling the three reunited duchies of Latvia. The shield is held by a red lion and a silver griffin.

ARMS OF LATVIA

Three stars for the
reunited duchies

The red lion
represents the
Duchy of Kurzeme

Rising sun
represents the
Duchy of Latgale

The silver griffin
recalls the Duchy of
Vidzeme

LITHUANIA

Ratio: *1:2*   Adopted: *March 20, 1989*   Usage: *National and Civil*

Yellow represents wheat and freedom from want

Green symbolizes the forests and renewed hope

Red symbolizes patriotism and courage

EUROPE

AFTER DECLARING independence from Russia in 1918, Lithuania was again occupied by the Soviet Union in 1940. It declared independence in 1991.

The national flag dates from the independent republic of 1918–1940. It was suppressed under the Soviet regime, but was readopted in 1990. Yellow is said to stand for ripening wheat, green for the forests, and red for love of the country, or alternatively for the blood shed in defense of the nation. Red also refers to the color of the medieval banners of the kingdom of Lithuania. Together, the colors stand for hope, courage, and freedom from want.

ARMS OF LITHUANIA
The coat of arms' red shield dates from the 14th century. It was re-adopted in 1991.

ARMS OF LITHUANIA

A white knight on his charger

The double-barred cross commemorates the conversion of Grand Duke Jaggelon of Lithuania to Catholicism in 1386, at the time of his marriage to Queen Hedwig of Poland

118

POLAND

Ratio: *5:8*   Adopted: *August 1, 1919*   Usage: *National*

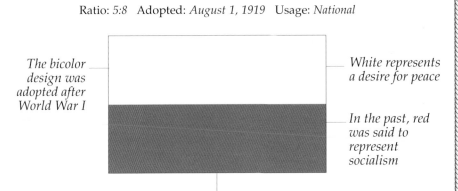

The bicolor design was adopted after World War I

White represents a desire for peace

In the past, red was said to represent socialism

Red and white were taken from the 13th-century arms

POLAND IS strategically placed in Europe, and its borders have constantly shifted. They were last altered in 1945, after World War II.

The red and white colors of the flag have been used since the 13th century, although they did not became the official national colors until 1831. They were taken from the colors of the national arms, first recorded in 1228.

THE NATIONAL ARMS

The coat of arms traditionally shows a white eagle on a red field. This emblem has remained more or less unchanged throughout Poland's turbulent history. The coat of arms was used by the Kingdom of Poland until its fall in 1795 and was re-adopted by the newly-declared republic around 1918/19, when a zigzag border and crown were added. The border and the crown were both dropped under the Communist administration; the crown was restored in 1993.

THE PEOPLE'S REPUBLIC OF POLAND

Under Communist rule from 1945–1989, white was commonly said to represent the people's desire for peace; during this period, red stood for socialism. The flag was re-confirmed as the national flag by the new government in 1992.

The plain bicolored flag is used for general purposes on land. When at sea, the flag is charged with the state arms in the center. Poland also has a swallow-tailed ensign, which is also charged with the state arms.

GERMANY

Ratio: *3:5*   Adopted: *May 23, 1949*   Usage: *National and Civil*

The colors of the German flag were taken from the uniforms of German soldiers during the Napoleonic Wars

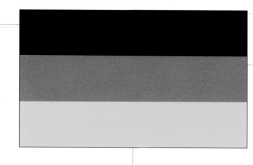

The flag was officially adopted for the republic in 1919

The flag was first adopted in 1848

· EUROPE

IN 1919 THE GERMAN EMPIRE became a republic. In 1949 it was divided into East and West Germany. In 1990 the two halves reunited.

Until the 19th century, Germany was a collection of feudal states. In 1848 an attempt was made to unite them, and although no union was established, a flag was produced. This was a black, red, and gold horizontal tricolor. The colors were taken from the uniforms of the German soldiers in the Napoleonic Wars in the late 18th century.

THE GERMAN EMPIRE
Most of the states finally united into the German Empire in 1871, but instead of retaining the black, red, and gold flag, the rival Bismarck tricolor of black, white, and red was adopted. This was a combination of the red of the Hanseatic League and the black and white of Prussia, of which Bismarck was Chancellor.

THE WEIMAR REPUBLIC
After Germany's defeat in World War I, a republic was declared in 1919 and the black, red, and gold flag returned. Its revival was short-lived, and in 1933 when the Nazi government came to power they restored the imperial colors and made their party flag, the *Hakenkreuz,* the national flag.

After World War II, both German states reverted to using the black, red, and gold tricolor, but East Germany added its coat of arms. Since reunification, the plain tricolor has been used.

Germany – Länder flags

ON GERMAN REGIONAL FLAGS the arms only appear on the official versions (except Lower Saxony, Saarland, and Rhineland Palatinate).

BADEN-WÜRTTEMBURG

The flag was adopted in 1953. Its colors derive from the arms of Duke Frederick V of Swabia. The coat of arms dates back to 1265. It was adopted as the state arms in 1954.

BAVARIA

Bavaria's flag was adopted in 1950, but blue and white have been Bavarian colors since 1330. The lozenge shapes first appeared on banners in the 15th century.

BERLIN

The flag was first adopted for West Berlin in 1950 and extended to the whole city in 1991. The bear, a pun on the name Berlin, dates from 1338 and the colors from 1861.

BRANDENBURG

The colors of the flag are from the shield, dating from 1170, although red and white were also the colors of the medieval Hanseatic League. The flag was adopted in 1990.

BREMEN

The flag of Bremen predates its coat of arms, which was adopted in 1891. Prior to this, Bremen was a member of the Hanseatic League, where the flag originated.

HAMBURG

Used since 1325, red and white are the Hanseatic colors. The castle is for Hamburg; the three towers for the Trinity; the cross for Christ; the stars for the Father and Holy Spirit.

HESSEN

The flag of Hessen was adopted 1948. The coat of arms was that of Ludwig III of Thuringia in 1182. The red and white colors of the flag are taken from the lion in the arms.

LOWER SAXONY

This flag uses the national flag with Lower Saxony's local arms in the center. It was adopted in 1946, but the arms dates from 1361, when it appeared on the seal of the ruler.

MECKLENBURG-
VORPOMMERN

This flag, adopted in 1991, combines blue and white of Pomerania with blue, yellow, and red of Mecklenburg. The bull and the gryphon are also local emblems. Red and white recall the Hanseatic League.

NORTH-RHINE-
WESTPHALIA

The coat of arms depicts the Rhine River of the Rhineland, the horse of Westphalia, and the rose of Lippe – the three territories that united to form the the state. The colors of the flag are from the arms.

RHINELAND-
PALATINATE

The flag was adopted in 1948 when the arms were placed on the national flag. The coat of arms depicts the lion of the Palatinate dating from 1229, the cross of Trier from 1273, and the wheel of Mainz from 1335.

SAARLAND

Adopted in 1957, the flag of Saarland recalls the different parts of the state. Depicted on the shield is the lion of Saarbrücken, the cross of Trier, the eagles of Lorraine, and the lion of Pfalz-Zweibrücken.

SAXONY

The flag was adopted in 1991, but the coat of arms is the traditional arms of the rulers of Saxony: black and yellow bands and the green crown of rue. The white and green flag dates from the 19th century.

SAXONY-ANHALT

This flag was the same as Baden-Württemberg until 1991, when the colors were reversed. The eagle recalls Prussia; the bicolored bands and rue crown, Saxony; and the bear and wall are the arms of Anhalt.

SCHLESWIG-
HOLSTEIN

The shield depicts two lions from arms of Schleswig and a nettle-leaf from those of Holstein. The colors of the flag, adopted in 1957, are taken from the arms.

THURINGIA

Another flag whose colors are based on the state arms. It was adopted in 1991. The red and white lion was the arms of the Counts of Thuringia in the 12th century.

THE NETHERLANDS

Ratio: 2:3   Adopted: *February 19, 1937*   Usage: *National and Civil*

Blue and white, along with the original orange, were the livery colors of William of Orange

In the mid-17th century, red, rather than orange, was made the official color

EUROPE

NETHERLANDS

Belgium   Germany

INDEPENDENT FROM SPAIN in the 16th century, the Netherlands was a republic until the Napoleonic Wars and became a kingdom in 1814.

The first *Stadtholder*, or ruler, of the Dutch Republic was William of Orange, who joined with Dutch nationalists and led the struggle for independence from Spain.

THE *PRINSVLAG*
Partly out of respect for him, the first flag adopted by the Dutch was a horizontal tricolor of orange, white, and blue *(see page 6)*. It became known as the *Prinsvlag* and was based on the livery of William of Orange. The orange dye was particularly unstable and tended to turn red after a while, so in the mid-17th century, red was made the official color. The flag has flown since then, but was confirmed by

Royal Decree only in 1937. As the first revolutionary flag, it has had a seminal influence throughout the world, particularly on the Pan-Slavic colors of Russia.

Until about 1800, in the case of both the orange- and red-striped versions, the number of stripes and their order frequently varied.

ARMS OF THE NETHERLANDS
The Dutch coat of arms depicts a golden lion on a blue shield, holding a sword and a sheaf of arrows. It is a combination of the coat of arms of the Dutch Republic and that of the House of Orange. The seven arrows represent the seven original provinces in the Netherlands.

The Netherlands – Provincial flags

Except for North Brabant and South Holland, the Dutch provincial flags are all modern creations.

DRENTHE

White and red are the colors of the Archbishops of Utrecht, former rulers of Drenthe. The black castle and stars recall the uprising of Coevorden against the Archbishop.

FLEVOLAND

Blue is for the Lake Ijssel from which the province was reclaimed. Green is for vegetation and yellow for the cornfields. The lily recalls Lely, the engineer of the reclamation project.

FRIESLAND

The flag is based on that of the 15th century kings of Friesland. The colors are those of the Dutch flag. The stripes and flowers represent the seven districts of Friesland.

GELDERLAND

In 1371, the dukedoms of Gelre and Gulik were united and combined their arms. The new arms was blue, yellow, and black, the colors that appear in the flag, hoisted in 1953.

GRONINGEN

The flag, adopted in 1950, combines green and white from the town of Groningen, surrounded by red, white, and blue of Ommeland, reflecting the town's position.

LIMBURG

The red lion is from the arms of Limburg. White and yellow are from local coats of arms, while the narrow blue stripe is for the Maas River which crosses the province.

NORTH BRABANT

The design, adopted in 1959, originated in Antwerp, where red and white checkered coats of arms were popular. It was associated with the area from the 17th century.

NORTH HOLLAND

Adopted in 1958, this flag unites the colors of Holland: yellow and red with the blue and yellow of West Friesland. Yellow, the common color, is placed at the top.

OVERIJSSEL

The yellow and red stripes recall the ancient association of this province with Holland. The wavy blue stripe running across the center is for the Ijssel River, after which the province is named.

SOUTH HOLLAND

The flag is a banner of the arms of Holland and was adopted in this form in 1986, replacing the previous simple triband of yellow-red-yellow, which was also based on the colors of the arms .

UTRECHT

The Archbishop of Utrecht used a red flag with a white cross from 1528. The Archbishop's flag remains in the canton of the modern flag, adopted in 1952. The field is in the traditional colors of the province.

ZEELAND

The flag of Zeeland, adopted in 1949, shows its full coat of arms. The wavy blue and white stripes are for the sea and the constant struggle to control it. From the water, the Dutch lion rises in triumph.

ARUBA

The flag of Aruba was adopted in 1976 when the island was still administered as part of the Netherlands Antilles. The flag was retained when Aruba became autonomous in 1986.

NETHERLANDS ANTILLES

Originally adopted in 1959, the flag incorporated the Dutch colors with six stars on the blue stripe for the island groups. These were reduced to five in 1986 when Aruba left the Netherlands Antilles.

BELGIUM

Ratio: *13:15* Adopted: *January 23, 1831* Usage: *National and Civil*

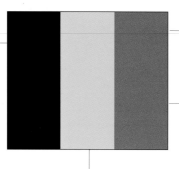

Black is taken
from the shield
of the arms

Red is adapted
from the lions
claws and tongue

The vertical layout
is derived from the
French Tricolore

Gold is the color of the lion in
the arms

EUROPE

FOLLOWING CENTURIES of foreign domination,
Belgium finally gained international recognition
as an independent kingdom in 1830.

Black, yellow, and red have been the colors of Belgium since before independence. They were derived from the coat of arms of Brabant, which depicts a black shield and a gold lion with red tongue and claws. The first flag in these colors was raised in 1792, during an attempt to gain Belgian independence from Austria, but the stripes were then horizontal. They were changed to the vertical position, after independence in 1831, in imitation of the French *Tricolore,* which represented liberty and revolution. They have remained unchanged ever since.

Belgian Regional flags

BRUSSELS

Adopted in 1991, the lily was widespread in the area that later became Brussels.

FLANDERS

Adopted in 1985, it is based on the arms, and the colors are taken from the national flag.

WALLONIA

The cockerel is derived from the Gallic cock, recalling the cultural links with France.

IRELAND

Ratio: *1:2*   Adopted: *January 21, 1919*   Usage: *National and Civil*

Green represents Catholics

Orange is for Protestant

White is for the union between Catholics and Protestants

EUROPE

AFTER CENTURIES of British rule, Ireland was split in 1921, becoming the Free State (Republic of Ireland) and the northern Six Counties.

The Irish flag is modeled on that of the French *Tricolore*. It was first flown by nationalists during their struggle for freedom from Britain in 1848, a year of Europe-wide revolution. But it was not until the Easter Rising of 1916 that it came to be regarded as the national flag. It was officially confirmed in 1919 and was written into the Constitution in 1937. The green coloring on the flag represents the Catholic majority; orange is for the Protestant minority (originally supporters of William of Orange), and white is for peace between the two faiths.

THE PRESIDENT'S STANDARD
The flag of the President was introduced in 1945 and is based on the ancient "Green Flag," a traditional symbol of Irish nationalism.

THE PRESIDENT'S STANDARD

The harp is said to be the harp of Brian Boru, an 11th-century ruler

The flag is similar to the quartering for Ireland on the Royal Arms of the United Kingdom

UNITED KINGDOM

Ratio: *1:2*   Adopted: *January 1, 1801*   Usage: *National and Civil*

The white saltire on a blue field was taken from the St. Andrew's Cross of Scotland

The saltire of Ireland's St. Patrick has been counter-changed with the white saltire of St. Andrew

The central red cross, fimbriated with white was adapted from England's St. George's Cross

EUROPE

THE UNITED KINGDOM was formed in 1707, uniting England, Scotland, and Wales. In 1801 Ireland joined, but in 1921 the south broke away.

The Union Flag is probably one of the world's best known flags, partly due to its unusual design, but more important, because of the importance of the British Empire in World history.

THE FIRST UNION FLAG
When King James of Scotland became King of England in 1603, both countries retained their own flags. Even today, the St. George's Cross and St. Andrew's Cross remain the flags of England and Scotland, respectively. In 1606 King James considered it necessary to have a flag reflecting the new union of Scotland and England and ordered that a Union Flag, more commonly known

as the Union Jack, be flown on British ships, combining the English Cross of St. George with the Scottish Cross of St. Andrew.

A NEW UNION FLAG
In 1801, when Ireland joined the Union, the so-called Cross of St. Patrick was added to form the present flag, but was counterchanged with the Cross of St. Andrew.

A ROYAL FLAG
The Union Flag was established as a maritime flag, and it remains a royal flag, not officially a national flag. The right of British citizens to fly the Union Jack on land must still be granted by royal permission.

UK – Subnational flags

MOST REGIONAL FLAGS are older than the Union Flag, except those based on the St. George's Cross, which date from the 20th century.

 ENGLAND

Originally used in 1191, the flag of St. George became the flag of England after 1277. The white flag has a red upright cross throughout. At sea it is the flag of an Admiral.

 WALES

Approved in 1959 as the Welsh national flag, the Red Dragon is an ancient emblem of Wales. For a time it appeared on a green hill, but the horizontal division is traditional.

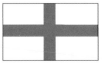 SCOTLAND
(The Standard)

The red lion on gold is the traditional royal flag of Scotland. The *fleur-de-lis* on the border recall the "auld alliance" with France. Its exact date of adoption is not known.

 SCOTLAND
(National flag)

In use since 1512, the Scottish flag is the Cross of St. Andrew. Because James was King of Scotland before he was King of England, this flag formed the basis of the Union Flag.

 ISLE OF MAN

Again, this is a traditional design. It was adopted in 1968. The *Trinacria*, three legs of Man, has been used for several centuries in varying forms, but its origin is uncertain.

 GUERNSEY

Guernsey formerly used only the Cross of St. George. In 1985 a gold cross, taken from the flag of William the Conqueror at the Battle of Hastings, was added to the flag.

 JERSEY

Prior to the adoption of its current flag, Jersey used a red diagonal cross on white, which is the same as the saltire of St. Patrick. The arms were added in 1981.

UK – Royal Standards

LIKE OTHER MONARCHIES, the UK has a wide range of flags that are armorial or semi-armorial for the leading members of its royal family. In the case of the Queen it is necessary to distinguish between her role as Queen of the United Kingdom and her other Realms, and as Head of the Commonwealth. In addition to her British Royal Standard, she has standards for other Realms.

ROYAL STANDARD OF THE UNITED KINGDOM

This form has been in use since the accession of Queen Victoria in 1837 and depicts the three areas united to form the United Kingdom (England, Scotland, and Ireland). Strictly, flags of this kind are armorial banners rather than "standards."

QUEEN AS HEAD OF THE COMMONWEALTH

This is used when the Queen is not in a Queen's Realm (i.e. a country of which she is directly the Head of State) or in one that does not have a local Royal Standard. It is a banner with Her Majesty's initial "E," a gold crown, and chaplet of roses.

PRINCE PHILIP DUKE OF EDINBURGH

The banner for Prince Philip has quarters representing his descent from the royal families of both Denmark and Greece, and from the Mountbattens; his title of Duke of Edinburgh is represented by the arms of the city.

PRINCE CHARLES

The banner is an adaptation of the Royal Standard, with a "label" for an eldest son, a white bar with three points, and the quartered arms of the Principality of Wales over all in the center. Labels are used for children and grandchildren of the Queen.

PRINCE CHARLES FOR USE IN WALES

For personal visits to Wales and as his own flag, the Prince uses the banner of the Principality of Wales with his crown on a green shield over all in the center. The Prince also has banners for his titles in Cornwall, Rothesay, and as Lord of the Isles.

OTHER ROYAL STANDARDS

Other members who have standards based on the Royal Standard are the Queen Mother, the Princess Royal, Princess Margaret, the Duke of York, Prince Edward, and the Queen's royal cousins. There is a general banner for those members of the royal family not entitled to an individual standard.

UK – Overseas Territories

OFFICIAL FLAGS for British Overseas Territories are generally based on the British blue or government ensign with a local badge in the fly.

 ANGUILLA

 ANGUILLA (Unofficial)

The flag of Anguilla was adopted in 1990. It is a blue ensign with the badge of the island. This derives from the unofficial flag used locally on land only.

Adopted in 1967, when the island separated from St. Kitts and Nevis. The turquoise stripe represents the sea, and the three dolphins are for friendship, wisdom, and strength.

 BERMUDA

 BRITISH VIRGIN ISLANDS

Bermuda uses an unusual red ensign. The badge shows a lion holding a shield on which appears the 1609 wreck of a ship, which struck a reef, not a cliff as is shown.

The badge dates from 1909, the flag from 1956. It shows St. Ursula, the namesake of the islands, with a lamp. She was martyred with 11,000 virgins, represented by 11 lamps.

 BRITISH ANTARCTIC TERRITORY

 BRITISH INDIAN OCEAN TERRITORY

The white field of the new flag, approved in 1998, symbolizes the snow which covers the Antarctic continent. It is used by research stations within the territory.

The flag was adopted in 1990. Blue and white wavy lines represent the ocean, and the palm recalls the natural vegetation of the islands. The crown shows British possession.

 CAYMAN ISLANDS

 FALKLAND ISLANDS

Blue and white lines recall the sea and the three stars, the three main islands. The lion of England appears above and the crest is a turtle and a pineapple for the fauna and flora.

The badge shows a ram for the sheep industry of the islands. The ship is the *Desire*, the ship of John Davies, who discovered the islands in 1592. The flag was hoisted in 1948.

GIBRALTAR
(Ensign)

GIBRALTAR
(City)

The blue ensign of Gibraltar was officially adopted in 1895. The badge is based on the arms of Gibraltar granted by Ferdinand, the King of Spain, in 1502. The castle and key recall that Gibraltar is not only a fortress but, because of its position on one side of a narrow strait, also the key to the Mediterranean Sea.

The local flag of Gibraltar City is a banner of the arms officially granted in 1926. It is based on the original arms granted by Spain in 1502. The banner was granted for use exclusively on land in 1983. Like the badge, it depicts a red fortress with a gold key. The red and white field is derived from the arms.

MONTSERRAT

PITCAIRN
ISLANDS

The coat of arms dates from 1909, although its origin is unknown. It shows a woman in green holding a cross and a harp. The cross is for Christianity, and the woman and harp recall Irish immigrants who settled on the island in 1632. The arms were readopted in 1962 when the West Indies Federation was dissolved.

Adopted for the Pitcairn Islands in 1984, the badge commemorates the island's earliest settlers, the infamous crew of the HMS *Bounty* who mutinied in 1790. The badge is blue to represent the Pacific Ocean, with a green triangle symbolizing the island. The shield is charged with the Bible and the anchor of HMS *Bounty*.

ST. HELENA

TURKS AND
CAICOS
ISLANDS

The current badge was made into a coat of arms in 1984. It depicts a ship flying the Cross of St. George sailing between two cliffs. Above is a wirebird representing the local fauna. The flag is also flown in the Ascension Islands and Tristan da Cunha, dependencies administered by St. Helena.

The blue ensign was granted in 1968, three years after the arms. The shield from the arms shows a conch shell and a crayfish representing fishing, the islands' main industry, and a cactus for their flora. The Turks and Caicos became a separate colony after the Bahamas achieved independence.

FRANCE

Ratio: *2:3* Adopted: *February 15, 1794* Usage: *National and Civil*

Red, white, and blue have come to represent liberty, equality, and fraternity – the ideals of the French Revolution

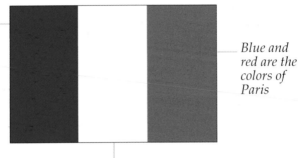

Blue and red are the colors of Paris

White is the color of the House of Bourbon

FRANCE WAS A MONARCHY until the the Revolution of 1789. A republic was created in 1792, following the abolition of the monarchy.

The traditional emblem of France was the *fleur-de-lis*, or lily, which first appeared on the arms in the 12th century.

A REVOLUTIONARY FLAG
The *Tricolore* was used during the Revolution and has since become a symbol of liberty around the world.

Other nations have also adopted the design. Because France has no arms, the *Tricolore* is also the national emblem.

The colors are probably derived from those of Paris, combined with those of the Bourbon Dynasty, though they are usually associated with liberty, equality, and fraternity.

Overseas Territories

CORSICA

Corsica flies a heraldic flag featuring a black Saracen's head on a white field. It is the emblem of the Corsican separatists.

FRENCH POLYNESIA

Red and white are local colors. The emblem depicts a *pirogue* – a local canoe – below a rising sun. The five crew recall the five island groups.

LUXEMBOURG

Ratio: *3:5* Adopted: *1848* Usage: *National*

The blue stripe is paler than that of the Netherlands

The colors date back to the 13th century

EUROPE

FOR MOST OF THE 19TH CENTURY Luxembourg was part of the Netherlands. It gained independence in 1890 and is Europe's last independent duchy.

Luxembourg had no flag until 1830, when patriots were urged to display the national colors. The flag was defined as a horizontal tricolor of red, white, and blue in 1848, but it was not officially adopted until 1972. The tricolor flag is almost identical to that of the Netherlands, except that it is longer and its blue stripe is a lighter shade. The red, white, and blue coloring was derived from the Grand Duke's coat of arms, which dates from the 13th century.

THE CIVIL ENSIGN
Since 1972 a banner of the Grand Duke's arms has been used as a civil ensign for use at sea. This is a blue and white striped field with a lion rampant in the center.

LUXEMBOURG CIVIL ENSIGN

Red, white, and blue coloring gave rise to colors of national flag

A crowned two-tailed lion rampant

MONACO

Ratio: *4:5*   Adopted: *April 4, 1881*   Usage: *National and Civil*

The bicolor design is common on other national flags, for example San Marino. It is often used as a background for heraldic livery

Red and white are the heraldic colors of the Grimaldi family

EUROPE

THE GRIMALDIS, a Genoese family, have ruled Monaco since the 13th century. Until 1860, the principality was considered part of Italy.

The present bicolor design was adopted in 1881 under Prince Charles III. It is identical to the far younger Indonesian national flag except in its statutory proportions, which are 4:5, compared to 2:3.

The Grimaldi coat of arms, which appears on the state flag, is the traditional one of the princely family and consists of a shield supported by two monks bearing swords. The device alludes to the legend of 1297, in which the Grimaldis conquered Monaco after entering the city with soldiers disguised as monks. Earlier Monegasque flags incorporated the Grimaldi shield and crown on a white field.

ARMS OF GRIMALDIS

A princely crown

The collar of the Order of St. Charles surrounds a shield of red and white (or silver)

The Grimaldi motto Deo Juvante *("With God's Help")*

ANDORRA

Ratio: 2:3   Adopted: *July 10, 1996*   Usage: *National and Civil*

The colors reflect Andorra's dependence upon France and Spain

Red and yellow are taken from the colors of Spain

Andorran coat of arms

Blue and red are taken from the colors of France

EUROPE

France

ANDORRA

Spain

THE PRINCIPALITY OF ANDORRA is an independent republic in the Pyrenees, between France and Spain. It is one of the world's oldest states.

The principality of Andorra has been under Franco-Spanish protection since 1278, governed by the Counts of Foix and the Bishops of Urgel. The colors of its national flag reflect France, blue and red; and Spain, yellow and red. The Andorran coat of arms is placed in the middle of the yellow stripe.

ARMS OF ANDORRA

Like the colors of the flag, the coat of arms also depicts the areas on which Andorra has been dependent. The quartered shield represents Urgel by the crozier and miter, Foix by the three vertical red stripes, Catalonia by the four vertical red stripes, and Béarn by the two cows.

ARMS OF ANDORRA

The crozier and miter symbolize the Bishops of Urgel

The four red stripes are taken from the arms of Catalonia

The three red stripes recall the Counts of Foix

The two cows are taken from the arms of Béarn

The motto is Virtus Unita Fortior – *"Strength united is stronger"*

PORTUGAL

Ratio: *2:3* Adopted: *June 30, 1911* Usage: *National and Civil*

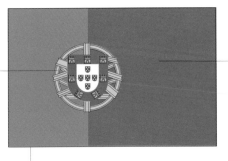

The armillary sphere – an early navigational tool

Red represents revolution

Green represents a Portuguese explorer, King Henry the Navigator

EUROPE

DURING THE 15th and 16th centuries, Portugal played a leading role in discovering the world beyond Europe. It formed a republic in 1910.

With the republic came a new flag. Portugal's old blue and white flag was replaced by a red and green one, representing revolution in red and Portuguese exploration in green.

AN IMPERIAL PAST
The central emblem symbolizes episodes from Portugal's imperial past. The white shield recalls King Afonso Henriques, who established Portugal as an independent kingdom. The seven gold castles stand for Portugal's expansion as a result of Alphonso's marriage in 1146. Behind the shield is an armillary sphere, which was an early navigational tool.

EMBLEM OF PORTUGAL

This armillary sphere and shield appear in the center of the Portuguese coat of arms

The seven gold castles stand for Portuguese expansion

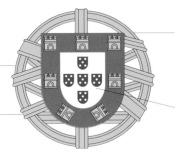

The armillary sphere recalls the importance of Portuguese exploration of the globe

The blue shields represent King Afonso Henriques

SPAIN

Ratio: 2:3   Adopted: *July 19, 1927*   Usage: *National and Civil*

Red and yellow are the colors of the arms of both Castille and Aragón

The first red and yellow flag of Spain was adopted in the 18th century for use at sea

The present layout was adopted in 1975

EUROPE

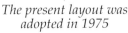

SPAIN WAS UNITED in the 15th century and rapidly became an imperial power. It lost most of its colonies during the 19th century.

Early Spanish flags were mostly heraldic; some, like the flag of Castilla y León *(see page 140)* survive today.

In 1785 the King of Spain adopted the red and yellow to distinguish his ships from those of other countries. The combination of colors was used by no other country, and although the present design was not adopted until 1927, they have always been associated with Spain. The colors were taken from the red and gold arms of both Castile and Aragón, the two regions united by King Ferdinand and Queen Isabella.

THE SPANISH REPUBLIC
When Spain became a republic in 1931, a new flag was adopted. This was an equal horizontal tricolor of red, yellow, and purple. The purple is thought to have referred to the arms of either León or Granada. However, when General Franco overthrew the republic in 1939, the original colors were restored.

THE NATIONAL ARMS
For state purposes the flag has the national arms set toward the hoist. The arms reflects the regions of Spain. The first and fourth quarters of the shield combine quarters representing Castile and León. The others recall Aragón and Navarre. In the base is the pomegranate of Granada. The whole shield is supported by the Pillar of Hercules.

Spain – Regional flags

ALTHOUGH MOST OF THE flags were adopted recently, all are based on older models, or traditional arms, displaying continuity with the past.

ANDALUSIA

Adopted in 1918, but not confirmed until 1983, the colors are those used during the Napoleonic Wars. The coat of arms depicts the Pillars of Hercules and the lions of Cadiz.

ARAGÓN

The stripes of Aragón date from the 14th century. Tradition states that a King of Aragón drew bloodstained fingers over a gold shield. The flag was adopted in 1981.

ASTURIAS

Blue is the color of the Virgin Mary. The cross is the Cross of Victory, a traditional Asturian emblem. From it hang Greek letters, the alpha and the omega, symbolizing Christ.

BALEARES

The field is the same as the flag of Aragón, to which the islands belonged in medieval times. The canton is the emblem of Palma de Majorca, the islands' capital.

THE BASQUE COUNTRY (PAÍS VASCO)

This flag was first adopted in 1931 and readopted in 1979. It is based on the Union Jack. Red recalls bloodshed, white, the Catholic faith, and green the Oak of Guérnica.

CANARY ISLANDS (ISLAS CANARIAS)

The colors symbolize those of the Virgin Mary and the Papacy. They are also thought to evoke the blue sea, the white beaches, and the golden sun. It was adopted in 1989.

CANTABRIA

White and red are the traditional colors of the area. The arms allude to the seafaring customs of the people and include an ancient seal. The flag was adopted in 1981.

CASTILLA-LA MANCHA

Adopted in 1989, the red stripe and the castle are the emblem of Castile. The white panel is intended to recall the surcoats worn by the soldiers in the Crusades.

CASTILLA Y LEÓN

This flag has been used by Castilla y León since 1248. It depicts the union of Castilla (castle) and León (lion). It was adopted for the region in 1989.

 EXTREMADURA

This flag was adopted in 1985, but the colors are traditional regional colors. Green is for fidelity, white for truth, and black for courage.

 LA RIOJA

The upper red stripe originally reflected the color of Rioja wine, but is now simply red. The colors are taken from the arms.

 MURCIA

The four castles recall Murcia's links with Castilla and the seven crowns, the seven regions of the province.

 VALENCIA

The stripes recall Valencia's links with Catalonia and the stylized crown, its period of independence.

 CATALONIA (CATALUNYA)

The flag, adopted in 1932, has been used since the 13th century and has the same origin as that of Aragón. It was outlawed from 1939 to 1975.

 GALICIA

Based on a traditional Galician design, white and blue are the colors of the Virgin Mary. The arms reflects loyalty to the Catholic Church.

 MADRID

The flag, adopted in 1983, is in the traditional color of Castilla. The seven white stars, from the arms, are for the seven districts of the region.

 NAVARRE

The red field and golden chains of Navarre date from the 14th century. The current flag was adopted in 1982.

ITALY

Ratio: *2:3*   Adopted: *June 18, 1946*   Usage: *National*

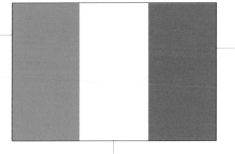

The first vertical tricolor was used until 1802; it was readopted in 1861

Green was said to be Napoleon's favorite color

White was added to distinguish it from the Mexican flag

EUROPE

ITALY WAS A COLLECTION of city states, dukedoms, and monarchies before it became a unified nation in 1861. Italy became a republic in 1946.

The Italian tricolor comes from the standard designed by Napoleon during the Italian campaign of 1796. The coloring was influenced by the French *Tricolore*, at first appearing in horizontal bands. The vertical tricolor was introduced in 1798, but was used only until the fall of Napoleon in 1814. It was re-introduced when the new Kingdom of Italy was formed in 1861. When the monarchy ended in 1946, the coat of arms of the House of Savoy was removed from the flag. The present flag was officially adopted in 1946.

ITALIAN CIVIL ENSIGN
The most famous seafaring states of ancient Italy are commemorated in the quarters of the civil ensign.

ITALIAN CIVIL ENSIGN

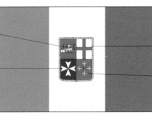

The winged lion of St. Mark represents Venice

The Maltese cross recalls Amalfi

The Cross of St. George represents Genoa

The Pisan cross stands for Pisa

MALTA

Ratio: *2:3*   Adopted: *September 21, 1964*   Usage: *National*

The George Cross
is fimbriated
with red

Red and white
were adapted from
the badge of the
Knights of Malta

EUROPE

MALTA WAS RULED successively by the Knights of
St. John of Jerusalem, by Napoleon, and by
Britain. It became independent in 1964.

A key stronghold during the
Crusades, much of the heraldry of
Malta is influenced by the colors and
devices of the Knights of Malta.
Their badge was the characteristic
Maltese cross, and their arms was a
white cross on a red field. From these
colors came the red and white shield
that was used during the colonial
period. The George Cross medal was
added to the shield in 1943. It was
awarded to the islanders by King
George VI of Britain for heroism in
World War II. In 1964, the blue
canton on which the cross was
originally placed was replaced by a
red fimbriation.

The President's flag, introduced in
1988, has the shield on a blue field,
with a Maltese cross in each corner.

THE PRESIDENT'S FLAG

The wreath of olive
and palm branches
represents peace

A gold mural crown
with a sally port and
eight turrets represents
fortifications of Valetta

The Maltese cross

The Shield of Malta

VATICAN CITY

Ratio: *1:1*   Adopted: *June 7, 1929*   Usage: *Civil*

Yellow (gold) and white (silver) are the colors of St. Peter's keys

The emblem features St. Peter's keys supporting the papal crown

Yellow and white were adopted as the Papal colors in 1808

EUROPE

VATICAN CITY, the Holy See of the Roman Catholic Church, is the smallest independent state in the world.

The modern Vatican colors were first adopted as the papal colors in 1808. The flag was used until 1870 when the Papal States were incorporated into a new unified Italy. In 1929, the Papal States were granted independent status, but their authority was confined to Vatican City. Gold and silver, represented in the flag as yellow and white, are the colors of the keys of St. Peter, which have accompanied papal arms since the Middle Ages. The flag's white stripe bears an emblem used since the 13th century to represent the Vatican's role as the headquarters of the Roman Catholic Church.

EMBLEM OF VATICAN CITY

The triple crown signifies the three types of temporal power – legislative, executive, and judicial – vested in the Pope

The crossed keys represent the keys to the Kingdom of Heaven bestowed by Christ on St. Peter

A red ropes binds the keys

SAN MARINO

Ratio: 4:5   Adopted: *April 6, 1862*   Usage: *National and Civil*

White represents the snow on Mt. Titano and the clouds above it

The colors are taken from the traditional arms, which is placed at the center of the flag for official purposes only

Blue recalls the sky

FOUNDED IN THE 4TH CENTURY, the Republic of San Marino is one of the smallest and oldest in the world. It lies on the slopes of Mt. Titano in Italy.

The flag of San Marino dates back to 1797 and was recognized by Napoleon as that of an independent state in 1799. The colors were taken from the coat of arms and were introduced in the 18th century. Blue is said to represent the sky over San Marino and white the clouds and snow on Mt. Titano.

The traditional coat of arms is placed in the center of the flag for official purposes only. It depicts three white towers crowned with ostrich plumes, representing three citadels resting on the peak of Mt. Titano, which was once vaned with ostrich feathers. They symbolize the state's ability to defend itself.

ARMS OF SAN MARINO

A wreath of laurel

The towers represent the three citadels, Guaita, Cesta, and Montale, situated on Mt. Titano

A wreath of oak leaves

The motto Libertas, *meaning "Liberty," also dates back to the 4th century, when the state was established as a refuge for those fleeing religious persecution*

144

SWITZERLAND

Ratio: *1:1*   Adopted: *December 12, 1889*   Usage: *National and Civil*

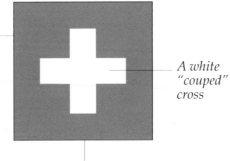

The red field with a white cross was adapted from the flag of Schwyz, one of the original three cantons

A white "couped" cross

This is the only square national flag (other than that of the Vatican)

EUROPE

IN 1291, A SMALL CONFEDERATION was formed to resist Austrian rule, beginning modern Switzerland. More cantons joined until 1815.

The flag of Switzerland is one of the most typical European flags. In medieval times many European states used a plain flag with a cross.

A FLAG FOR THE CONFEDERATION

For many years, the separate cantons of Switzerland had no one common flag but were each represented by their own flags. The present flag of Switzerland, a white "couped" cross on a red field, was based on that of Schwyz, one of the three original provinces that united into a confederation against the Holy Roman Empire in 1291. It became accepted as the common badge of the Confederation in 1339 at the Battle of Laupen, when it was used to distinguish the soldiers of the Confederation from other soldiers, and became the accepted flag of the Confederation in 1480. It was not officially confirmed as the flag of Switzerland until 1848 and it was last regulated in 1889.

Apart from that of the Vatican, the Swiss flag is the only totally square national flag. However, when used on the Swiss lakes, it has the ratio of 2:3; a practice adopted in 1941.

THE NATIONAL ARMS

The coat of arms is simply a shield in the form of the flag. It was officially adopted in 1889. Every town or commune in Switzerland has its own flag and coat of arms.

Switzerland – Canton flags

IN EVERY CASE the flags are based on the arms of the canton, some of which predate the canton's joining the Swiss Confederation.

AARGAU

Adopted in 1803, the white waves on black represent the Aare River, and the white stars on blue, the districts of Baden, the Free Areas, and Fricktal which came together to form the canton. In 1963 it was decreed that the stars should be arranged 2 and 1.

APPENZELL AUSSER-RHODEN

Adopted in 1597 when the canton separated from Inner-Rhoden, the flag retained the bear, but added the initials VR (for Ussroden). The bear dates back to medieval banners. It was used from 1403 onward in battles against feudal landlords.

APPENZELL INNER-RHODEN

This is the original form of the flag before the partition from Appenzell Ausser-Rhoden in 1597. The bear emblem was widely used in the Middle Ages, and was taken by the Appenzellers from the arms of the abbey of St. Gall.

BASEL-LAND

Basel-Land separated from the City in 1832. The arms and flag were adopted in 1834 based on the form of crozier used in Liestal, with the crook turned to the right and decorated with small spheres. This was made official in 1947.

BASEL-STADT

The emblem of Basel-Stadt is the headpiece of a bishop's crozier. The emblem dates back to the earliest days of heraldry. Since the 15th century it has been depicted as black on white. It was kept in this form when the canton was divided in 1832.

BERN

The coat of arms dates back to the 12th century. Soon afterward the arms, which depict a bear on a red field with a yellow diagonal, became the canton's banner. There have, however, been many variant forms through the ages. The bear represents the name of the canton.

FRIBOURG

The original colors of Fribourg, black and white, were readopted when it joined the Confederation in 1831, but date back to 1410 and are related to the coat of arms.

GLARUS

The flag of Glarus depicts the figure of St. Fridolin, the patron saint of the canton, on a red field. The flag was adopted when the canton joined the Confederation in 1352.

JURA

This flag was adopted 1978, when Jura became a separate canton. It was formerly part of Basel-Land – recalled by the crozier – and Bern. The stripes are from the arms of Jura.

NEUCHÂTEL

The tricolor adopted in 1848 is in traditional colors. The white cross was added to show the canton's association with Switzerland.

GENEVA

The eagle recalls the former Holy Roman Empire. The key is the Key of St. Peter, and shows Geneva as the key to western Switzerland. The flag was adopted in 1815.

GRAUBUNDEN

The flag includes symbols for the three original parts of the canton that united in the 15th century: Graubunden, Zehgerichtenbund, and the Gotteshausbund.

LUCERNE

Lucerne was the first canton, after the original three, to join the Confederation in 1332. Its flag has the colors of its shield arranged horizontally instead of vertically.

NIDWALDEN

The key with two wards is the emblem of St. Peter and was used in the 15th century. It was retained when the canton divided in 1815.

OBWALDEN

The key with only one ward was used in Obwalden starting in the 13th century, and it was this form that was adopted when the separate canton was formed in 1815.

SANKT GALLEN

The emblems of Sankt Gallen – an ax and a fasces – were adopted in 1803 when the canton was formed under French influence. They are both symbols of republicanism.

SCHAFFHAUSEN

The emblem has been in use since the 14th century. It depicts a ram (the "sheep" of the town's name) on a yellow field. The flag's existence was first recorded as early as 1386.

SCHWYZ

Schwyz was one of the first three cantons, and the one from which the country takes its name. Its arms existed before the Confederation was formed in 1291.

SOLOTHURN

The coat of arms dates back to 1394 and has colors derived from those of the Confederation. The flag was originally red with a white cross but was simplified into its current form.

THURGAU

The flag of Thurgau, adopted in 1803, depicts two gold lions arranged diagonally. They are taken from the coat of arms that dates from medieval times.

TICINO

The colors of Ticino's flag may be derived from the French *Tricolore*, or from the main colors of the arms of the united townships.

URI

The emblem is an auroch's head (linked to the canton's name). It dates from the 13th century, but the nose ring was added later.

VALAIS

The modern flag of Valais is derived from that of the original republic, which had seven stars for its component townships. These were increased to 12 in 1802 and retained when the state joined the Confederation in 1814.

VAUD

The colors date from 1798 when the Léman Republic was formed, and stand for freedom. They were retained when the state entered the Confederation in 1803. The motto is *Liberté et Patrie* ("Freedom and Fatherland").

ZUG

Zug joined the Confederation in 1352 and again in 1364, after a brief return to Habsburg rule. The colors of the flag were originally red-white-red of Austria, but were altered to the blue and white from the arms of the Counts of Lenzburg in 1352.

ZÜRICH

The flag in this case preceded the arms and dates back to the 13th century. It was adopted in 1351 when Zürich joined the Confederation. However, since 1957 it has been compulsory to depict the flag in the same format as the shield.

LIECHTENSTEIN

Ratio: *3:5* Adopted: *June 24, 1937* Usage: *National and Civil*

The yellow crown was introduced to distinguish Liechtenstein as a principality

Red and royal blue have been used to represent the country of Liechtenstein since the 18th century

THE PRINCIPALITY OF LIECHTENSTEIN was created in 1719 as part of the Holy Roman Empire. It gained full independence in 1806.

The red and blue of Liechtenstein's flag date from 1921. There was confusion at the 1936 Olympic Games in Berlin because the flag was very similar to that of Haiti. In 1937 the crown was introduced to the flag of Liechtenstein to establish the country's status as a principality and to distinguish it from the Haitian flag. The flag can be hung vertically or horizontally, but the crown always remains upright.

THE PRINCE'S FLAG
The arms of Silesia, Künringen, Troppau and East Friesland, and Rietburg make up the four quarters of the shield of the Prince's arms, in the center of his flag. They represent the noble ancestors of the prince.

THE FLAG OF PRINCE OF LIECHTENSTEIN

The inner shield represents the ancient princely family

Red and yellow are the Prince's colors

The four arms within the Prince's Arms represent his noble ancestors

150

AUSTRIA

Ratio: *2:3*   Adopted: *May 1, 1945*   Usage: *National and Civil*

According to legend, the red and white flag was modeled on the bloodstained surcoat of a Duke wounded in battle

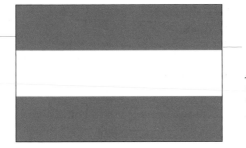

The traditional flag, retained after the fall of the Hapsburgs in 1918

EUROPE

AUSTRIA ONCE RULED much of central Europe, but lost most of its territory in 1919. Between 1938 and 1945 Austria was annexed to Germany.

Tradition states that a Duke of Austria once fought so fiercely in battle that the white tunic he wore was soaked in blood, except for the part covered by his swordbelt. So he adopted red with a white band across the center as his colors.

ONE OF THE WORLD'S OLDEST FLAGS
The story is probably apocryphal, but stripes of red-white-red have been an emblem of Austria for over 800 years. Their use on a flag was recorded in 1191, making the Austrian flag one of the world's oldest flags. It was officially adopted as the national flag after the fall of the Hapsburg Dynasty, and the formation of a republic in 1918.

During World War II, the Austrian flag and arms were banned, they were restored in 1945.

ARMS OF AUSTRIA
The coat of arms depicts an imperial black eagle, an emblem used by the Hapsburgs. It originally had two heads, but they were changed to one when the Hapsburg Empire disintegrated. On the eagle's chest is a shield in the national colors. The eagle holds a hammer and sickle, recalling agricultural and industrial workers. Its crown, with three turrets, also represents agriculture, industry, and commerce. The broken chains on the eagle's feet symbolize the restoration of freedom.

Austria – State flags

MOST PROVINCIAL FLAGS in Austria are based on the local arms. In many cases they existed before their official adoption.

BURGENLAND

The colors of the flag, officially hoisted in 1971, are based on the red eagle and yellow shield of the arms.

CARINTHIA

Adopted in 1946, the colors are derived from those of Austria and the yellow state shield.

LOWER AUSTRIA

Adopted in 1954, the colors are based on the arms which contain a blue shield and five gold eagles.

SALZBURG

The flag, adopted in 1921, uses the traditional colors of the state, based on the national colors.

STYRIA

The coat of arms of Styria is a green shield bearing a white lion. The flag, adopted in 1960, uses these colors.

TYROL

The bicolored flag is derived from the arms which depicts a red eagle on a white disk. It was adopted in 1945.

UPPER AUSTRIA

Upper Austria's flag, adopted in 1949, is derived from the national colors and the arms of the province.

VIENNA

The flag dates from 1946. It is based on the city's arms but is identical to the flags of Salzburg and Vorarlberg.

VORARLBERG

Like the flags of Salzburg and Vienna, Vorarlberg's bicolor flag is based on the provincial arms.

HUNGARY

Ratio: *2:3*   Adopted: *October 1, 1957*   Usage: *National and Civil*

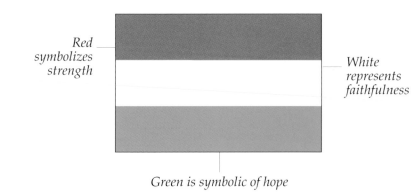

Red symbolizes strength

White represents faithfulness

Green is symbolic of hope

PART OF THE AUSTRO-HUNGARIAN EMPIRE until 1918, the nation was part of the Communist bloc from 1945–1989.

The current flag was first used in the 1848–49 uprising. Its pattern was derived from the French *Tricolore* used during the French Revolution. The colors: red, white, and green date back to the 9th century. They were first used in 1608 during the reign of King Matthias II. Until 1945, the royal crown appeared in the center of the national flag. During Hungary's brief period as a republic from 1945–1949, the royal crown was replaced by the *Kossuth* coat of arms. When the Communists took power, they added a Soviet-style emblem to the flag. In 1990, the arms of the kingdom were readopted, but they were not replaced on the flag.

ARMS OF HUNGARY

The red and white stripes probably originated from Spain in the late 12th or early 13th century

The crown of St. Stephen, the first king of Hungary

The patriarchal cross was added to the Hungarian arms about 800 years ago

153

CZECH REPUBLIC

Ratio: *2:3*   Adopted: *March 30, 1920*   Usage: *National and Civil*

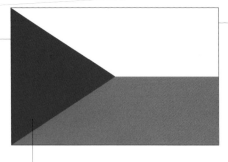

The blue triangle was added to distinguish the flag from that of Poland

White and red are the heraldic colors of Bohemia (any similarity to the Pan-Slavic colors is coincidental)

Blue represents the state of Moravia

EUROPE

THE CZECH REPUBLIC was part of Austria until 1919, when it merged with Slovakia to form Czechoslovakia. The states separated in 1993.

The first flag of Czechoslovakia was based on the arms, and was white over red. This was identical to the flag of Poland, so a blue triangle was added at the hoist. The flag was banned by the Nazis in 1938, and a horizontal tricolor of white, red, and blue was enforced. The original flag was restored in 1949.

THE NEW CZECH REPUBLIC

When the Czech Republic and Slovakia separated in 1993, the Czechs decided to keep their existing flag, recalling the two principal parts of the country.

The greater coat of arms depicts a quartered shield reflecting the regions of the Czech Republic.

GREATER ARMS OF THE CZECH REPUBLIC

The white lion on a red field is the traditional emblem of Bohemia

The black eagle on a yellow field is taken from the arms of Silesia

The red and white eagle on a blue field is from the arms of Moravia

The Bohemian arms are repeated to fill the shield

SLOVAKIA

Ratio: 2:3 Adopted: *September 1, 1992* Usage: *National and Civil*

The arms of
Slovakia

A version of
this flag was
first used in
the 19th
century

Red, white, and blue are
Pan-Slavic colors

UNDER HUNGARIAN RULE until 1919, Slovakia then formed part of Czechoslovakia with the Czech Republic. The two states separated in 1993.

The first Slovak flags, used during the 19th century, resembled the Russian flag, because the Slovaks looked to Russia for aid in gaining independence. As Czechoslovakia, a red and white flag with a blue triangle was used. During World War II, Slovakia re-adopted the white, blue, and red tricolor, with the arms in the center.

ARMS OF SLOVAKIA
The arms uses colors of the early flags, a white patriarchal cross rising from blue mountains on a red shield.

At independence in 1993, the red, white, and blue tricolor was retained as the national flag, but the arms was placed toward the hoist.

The President's flag has the arms, bordered by the national colors.

THE PRESIDENT'S FLAG

The flag is bordered
by stripes in the
national colors; red,
blue, and white

A patriarchal cross

A stylized image of
Slovakia's
mountains

SLOVENIA

Ratio: *1:2*   Adopted: *June 24, 1991*   Usage: *National and Civil*

The coat of arms was added in 1991 when Slovenia became independent

White, blue, and red are Pan-Slavic colors, popularized in the 19th century

The order of the tricolor is the same as the flag for Slovenia, when it was part of Yugoslavia

EUROPE

Austria
Italy SLOVENIA
Croatia

HISTORICALLY UNDER Austrian rule, Slovenia formed part of Yugoslavia in 1919. It declared independence on June 26, 1991.

Like Slovakia, Slovenia looked to Russia in the 19th century for assistance in gaining independence. For the same reason, the Pan-Slavic tricolor of blue, white, and red was adopted for Yugoslavia, with a gold fimbriated red star added by Tito in 1946. Slovenia also had its own flag within Yugoslavia, distinguished by the order of the stripes (white, blue, red). At independence Slovenia placed its arms in the upper hoist of this tricolor, to create a distinct national flag.

The arms depicts mountain peaks, above wavy blue lines symbolizing the sea coast. The stars are from the arms of the Duchy of Selje.

ARMS OF SLOVENIA

The three stars are from the arms of the former Duchy of Selje

The three mountain peaks represent the Triglav, part of the Alps

The wavy lines symbolize Slovenia's sea coast

CROATIA

Ratio: *1:2*   Adopted: *December 22, 1990*   Usage: *National and Civil*

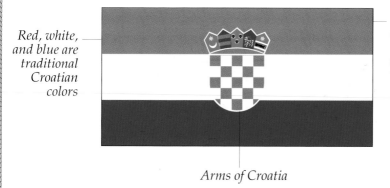

Red, white, and blue are traditional Croatian colors

The tricolor charged with the coat of arms was first used during World War II

Arms of Croatia

EUROPE

FOR MUCH OF ITS existence, Croatia was under Austrian rule. It joined Yugoslavia in 1919, but declared independence on June 25, 1991.

While part of Yugoslavia, Croatia's flag was designed in the Pan-Slavic colors: red, white, and blue. These are also traditional Croatian colors used in the 19th century.

During World War II, Croatia became a semi-independent state and added the arms of Croatia to the center of its flag. Following the war,

Croatia retained its tricolor, but a gold-edged red star was placed in the center by Tito. Before gaining independence, the present flag was adopted, based on the one used during the war.

The shield is in the red and white checks of Croatia. Above is a row of shields of its various territories.

ARMS OF CROATIA

The small shields at the top are taken from the arms of Croatia's regions

From left to right the shields represent the ancient arms of Croatia, Dubrovnik, Dalmatia, Istria, and Slavonia

The red and white checks are traditional emblems of Croatia

BOSNIA & HERZEGOVINA

Ratio: *1:2* Adopted: *February 4, 1998* Usage: *National and Civil*

The dark blue and yellow, and the stars, refer to the flag of Europe

The geographical shape of Bosnia is a triangle

The flag was imposed on the multiethnic country by the international High Representative

EUROPE

BOSNIA-HERZEGOVINA was under Turkish rule until it was ceded to Austria in 1878. From 1945 to 1992 it formed part of Yugoslavia.

After Bosnia-Herzegovina had broken away from Yugoslavia in 1992, a neutral plain white flag was adopted by parliament. The country's independence triggered a civil war between the three ethnic groups – Muslims, Croats, and Serbs. After the Dayton peace agreement was signed in 1995, the "neutral" Bosnian flag became unacceptable to the Croats and Serbs.

In February 1998, the international High Representative, who safeguards the peace in Bosnia-Herzegovina, imposed a new flag. However, it was designed by a committee with members from all three ethnic groups.

The country is now divided into two parts: the Bosnian-Croat Federation and the Serb Republic.

BOSNIA-CROAT FEDERATION FLAG

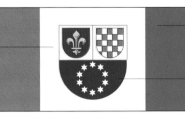

Green is the color of Islam

Red and white are Croatian colors

The ten stars are for the ten cantons in the Federation

SERBIA & MONTENEGRO

Ratio: *1:2*   Adopted: *April 27, 1992*   Usage: *National and Civil*

The order of the colors in the tricolor was used only for the national flag of Yugoslavia

Blue, white, and red are Pan-Slavic colors, adopted in the 19th century

In 2002 an agreement was signed with the aim of restructuring the Federal Republic of Yugoslavia, re-naming it as the Union of Serbia and Montenegro.

EUROPE

RULED BY TURKEY and Austria, a number of states united in 1919 to form Yugoslavia. In 1991, several areas declared independence.

Prior to its formation in 1919, nearly all the regions of Yugoslavia used red, white, and blue Pan-Slavic flags. To distinguish the national flag of Yugoslavia, the order of the stripes was made blue, white, and red, an arrangement not used by the other states. The plain flag was used for civil purposes on land and sea.

The state flag had the Royal Arms in the center.

After World War II, Yugoslavia became a Communist state under Marshall Tito, and the coat of arms was replaced by a gold-edged red "Partisan Star." After the breakup of the country in 1991, the star was removed.

INDIVIDUAL FLAGS

 MONTENEGRO

The flag is identical to Serbia's, except for its proportions. Prior to joining Yugoslavia, the Montenegrin flag bore a Royal Cipher. From 1946–1992 both contained gold-edged red stars.

 SERBIA

The Pan-Slavic flag has historically been used in Serbia. It is also used, in parts of Bosnia and Croatia inhabited by Serbs.

ALBANIA

Ratio: *5:7*   Adopted: *April 7, 1992*   Usage: *National*

The Albanians call their country Shapipëria, meaning "land of the eagle"

The traditional heraldic Albanian flag first used in 1912 when independence was restored

EUROPE

ONCE PART OF the Byzantine Empire, Albania became a kingdom in 1912. From 1944 to 1991 it was a strict Communist state.

The black eagle first appeared on the Albanian flag in the 15th century when Albania became part of the Byzantine Empire. According to legend, the Albanians are descendants of the eagle. The red flag, with the eagle in the center, was adopted in 1912, when independence was restored. Parts of the Italian arms were included on the flag after the invasion of 1939, but the original flag was restored in 1942.

In 1946, the flag changed again, to incorporate a gold-edged red star above the eagle, representing the Communist regime. The star was removed in 1991, by order of the new multiparty government.

ARMS OF ALBANIA

The black eagle has been an emblem of Albania since the 15th century

The two-headed eagle first appeared on flags used during the struggle against Turkish occupation

MACEDONIA

Ratio: *1:2*   Adopted: *October 5, 1995*   Usage: *National and Civil*

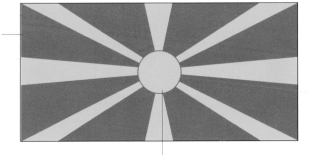

Red was the
traditional
color of the
Macedonian
flag

*The radiant sun was added in 1995 to
replace the controversial "Star of Vergina"*

MACEDONIA WAS under Turkish rule for centuries. It united with Serbia in 1913 and became part of Yugoslavia. It declared independence in 1992.

As part of Yugoslavia, Macedonia was the only region not to use the Pan-Slavic colors. Its flag was red with a gold-edged red star in the canton.

A CONTROVERSIAL NEW FLAG

At independence in 1992, Macedonia retained the red flag but added a gold star in a gold sun. This was soon changed to the Star of Vergina, an ancient Macedonian emblem from the tomb of Philip of Macedon, father of Alexander the Great. Greece objected to this, claiming the star as a Greek emblem. In 1995 the star was replaced by a radiant sun.

Macedonia's arms is similar in design to former Soviet emblems.

ARMS OF MACEDONIA

Symmetrical
wreaths of wheat

The star of
socialism

A radiant sun,
also used on
the national
flag

161

BULGARIA

Ratio: *3:5*   Adopted: *November 22, 1990*   Usage: *National and Civil*

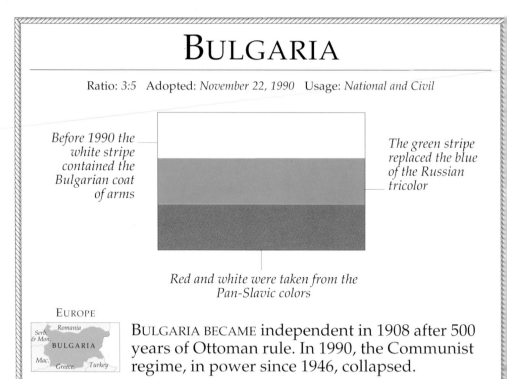

Before 1990 the white stripe contained the Bulgarian coat of arms

The green stripe replaced the blue of the Russian tricolor

Red and white were taken from the Pan-Slavic colors

Romania
Serb. & Mon.
BULGARIA
Mac.
Greece   Turkey

BULGARIA BECAME independent in 1908 after 500 years of Ottoman rule. In 1990, the Communist regime, in power since 1946, collapsed.

While under Turkish rule, Bulgaria had no national flag. When it became a principality in 1878, a slight variation of the Pan-Slavic colors was adopted. These colors were widely used during independence movements of the late 19th century, The horizontal arrangement of the tricolor was based on the Russian flag at the time, but for Bulgaria's national flag the central blue stripe was substituted by green.

THE PEOPLE'S REPUBLIC

No change was made to the flag during Bulgaria's period as an independent kingdom from 1908–1946, but with the formation of the People's Republic in 1947, a coat of arms was added in the white stripe near the hoist. This depicted a rampant lion; a red star representing Communism; and later a cogwheel symbolizing industrialization. The coat of arms was removed from the flag in 1990 because of its Communist connotations. No arms now appear on the flag.

THE SYMBOLISM OF THE COLORS

Although based on the Pan-Slavic colors, the white band is said to represent a love of peace, and red, the valor of the people. The green stripe, substituted for the traditional Pan-Slavic blue in 1878, was intended to represent the youthfulness of the emerging nation.

GREECE

Ratio: 2:3   Adopted: 1822   Usage: *National and Civil*

The cross in the canton represents Greek religious faith

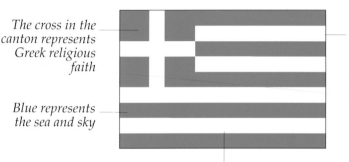

The nine stripes represent the nine syllables in the cry "Freedom or Death" uttered during the Greek war of independence

Blue represents the sea and sky

White reflects the purity of the Greek independence struggle

ONCE PART of the Ottoman Empire, Greece has seen periodic unrest since World War II. In 1974 it became a multiparty democracy.

The flag flown by Greece is in the same colors as the one that was raised following independence from the Ottoman Empire in the early 19th century. At various times since then, Greece has used a plain white cross on a blue background as its sea flag, and its land flag. Today the plain Cross Flag is preserved in the President's flag and in the canton of the blue-and-white-striped national flag.

The shade of blue of the flag has also varied. Today it is the original light blue color of 1822. It was altered in the 1970s, and the blue was changed to a much darker, navy shade.

THE PRESIDENT'S FLAG

The original white cross on a blue field is retained in the President's flag and the national arms

The Cross Flag is surrounded by a wreath of laurels

ROMANIA

Ratio: 2:3   Adopted: *December 27, 1989*   Usage: *National and Civil*

Blue formed part of the province of Moldova's flag

Red was featured in the flags of both Moldova and Wallachia and is the color of Romanian unity

Yellow formed part of the province of Wallachia's flag

EUROPE

ROMANIA EMERGED from the Ottoman Empire as an independent kingdom in 1859. It is now a democracy, after decades of Communist rule.

The current flag was created in 1848 by combining the colors of Wallachia and Moldova – the Ottoman provinces that made up Romania. In 1867 the Royal Arms was set in the yellow stripe. The coat of arms was modified many times, and in 1948 it was replaced with a Communist emblem. This was jettisoned following the fall of the Ceausescu regime in 1989.

NEW NATIONAL ARMS
In 1992, the old coat of arms was restored by the new parliament. It features a combination of motifs which recall Romania's past as a powerful medieval state.

ARMS OF ROMANIA

The eagle grips an Orthodox Christian cross in its beak

The sword recalls St. Stephen the Great of Moldova

The scepter of St. Michael the Brave of Wallachia

The smaller shield displays the arms of some of Romania's provinces

MOLDOVA

Ratio: *1:2*   Adopted: *May 12, 1990*   Usage: *National and Civil*

The arms of
Moldova

The blue, yellow, and red colors reflect
strong links with Romania

Ukraine
MOLDOVA
Romania

MOLDOVA WAS ONCE part of Romania but was
incorporated into the Soviet Union in 1940. It has
been fully independent since 1991.

The blue, red, and yellow tricolor of
Moldova is almost identical the
Romanian flag, reflecting the two
countries' cultural affinity.

ARMS OF MOLDOVA
On Moldova's flag the yellow stripe
is charged with the national arms.
Like the Romanian coat of arms, the

Moldovan arms, adopted in 1990,
features a golden eagle holding an
Orthodox Christian cross in its beak.
Instead of a sword, the eagle is
holding an olive branch. The blue
and red shield on the eagle's breast is
also different – on it are an ox head,
a star, a rose, and a crescent, all
traditional symbols of Moldova.

ARMS OF MOLDOVA

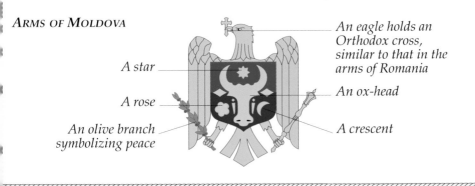

A star

A rose

An olive branch
symbolizing peace

An eagle holds an
Orthodox cross,
similar to that in the
arms of Romania

An ox-head

A crescent

BELARUS

Ratio: *1:2*   Adopted: *May 16, 1995*   Usage: *National and Civil*

A national ornament representing woven cloth

Red and green were the colors of Belarus's flag while it was a Soviet republic

Red and white are traditional Belarussian colors

EUROPE

BELARUS, formerly White Russia, became independent of the USSR in 1991, although its ties with Russia are increasing once more.

The original flag of Belarus while under Soviet administration in 1922 was similar to that of the USSR. It was changed in 1951, and the flag used today is similar to this second flag, except that the Communist hammer, sickle, and star have been removed, and the red and white portions of the hoist ornamentation have been reversed.

THE REJECTED DESIGN

Following independence from the USSR in 1991, Belarus adopted a flag of three equal horizontal stripes of white-red-white. This was the same flag that had been associated with a brief period of Belarussian independence in 1918, and its colors were derived from the arms of the republic. The design was rejected in a referendum in 1995.

The flag of Belarus, adopted following the referendum, reflects its growing ties with Russia. The unusual ornamentation in the hoist is described as a national ornament and represents woven cloth.

ARMS OF BELARUS

The Soviet-style coat of arms, retained on independence, also reflects the dominant Russian influence. This depicts an outline of the state against a sun rising from behind a globe. This is entirely surrounded by wreaths of wheat and flowers.

UKRAINE

Ratio: 2:3   Adopted: *September 4, 1991*   Usage: *National and Civil*

Originally the
flag of the
republic in 1918

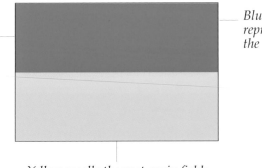

Blue
represents
the sky

Yellow recalls the vast grain fields

UKRAINE FORMED an independent state in 1918, but came under Soviet control one year later and remained so until independence in 1991.

The bicolored flag flown in Ukraine today was the official flag of the country in 1918 when Ukraine enjoyed a brief period of independence. With the invasion of the Red Army, the flag was suppressed until the German occupation of 1941–1944. After the war it was banned again by the Soviet Union. When Ukraine gained its independence in 1991 the country readopted its original flag. The blue is supposed to represent the sky and the yellow the vast fields of grain of the country's agriculture.

The Ukrainian coat of arms is in the national colors and features an ancient trident symbol.

ARMS OF UKRAINE

Blue and yellow are
national colors

The trident of
St. Volodimir

The trident is
an ancient
symbol dating
back to pre-
Roman times

RUSSIAN FEDERATION

Ratio: *2:3*   Adopted: *August 22, 1991*   Usage: *National and Civil*

The colors of the flag were adapted from the original flag of the Netherlands

Since its official adoption in 1799, the Russian tricolor has had a major influence on other east European flags

White, blue, and red are Pan-Slavic colors

RUSSIA WAS FORMED in the 15th century; by 1922, when the USSR was established, it encompassed much of Asia. The USSR collapsed in 1991.

At the end of the 17th century, Peter the Great of Russia visited western Europe. Following this visit he decided to adopt a variation of the Dutch flag as a civil ensign for Russian ships. This was a horizontal tricolor of white, blue, and red. It was only officially recognized in 1799. Peter the Great also adopted a flag for the Russian navy, which was white with the blue diagonal Cross of St. Andrew.

THE PAN-SLAVIC COLORS
Both the color and tricolor design of this first flag had a major influence on many of the flags of eastern European nations, which looked to Russia for help in liberating them from foreign domination during the 19th century. They have since become known as the Pan-Slavic colors.

THE HAMMER, SICKLE, AND STAR
After the Russian Revolution of 1917, the Communists abolished all former flags and instead adopted the Red Flag as the flag of the Soviet Union. This contained a gold hammer and sickle, symbols of the proletariat and the peasants, under a gold-edged red star, representing unity. As a Soviet republic, Russia used this flag with a vertical blue bar at the hoist.

When the Soviet Union collapsed in 1991, the former flags of Russia, including the white, blue, and red tricolor were restored.

Russian Federation – Republic flags

<small>UNLIKE MOST OTHER COUNTRIES,</small> the flags of the Russian republics are all new, adopted since 1991.

 ADYGEYA

Designed by a British traveler who helped resist annexation of the republic by Russia, the arrows are for resistance. Green is for agriculture and gold is for freedom.

 ALTAY

Blue represents the cleanliness of the sky, mountains, rivers, and lakes of Altay. White is for eternity, and to encourage the revival of love and harmony between the Altay people.

 BASHKORTOSTAN

Blue is for charity and virtue; white for openness and willingness; green for freedom and eternal life. The *kurai* flower represents the seven races of the Bashkir people.

 BURYATIYA

Blue is for the sky and water; white for purity; yellow for freedom and prosperity. The *Soembo* – the moon, sun, and hearth – recall reconciliation, family life, and hospitality.

 CHECHENIA

The colors of this flag represent traditional themes. Green is for Islam and also new life. Red recalls the blood shed for freedom, and white is the road leading to the future.

 CHUVASHIA

The red base is the Chuvash land, from which grows the Tree of Life. The three suns are an ancient Chuvash emblem. Gold is for the future and prosperity.

 DAGHESTAN

The upper green stripe is for agriculture and hope. The blue stripe is for the Caspian Sea which borders the republic. Red represents fidelity and courage.

 INGUSHETIA

The stripe is for the pure intentions and actions of the people, and green for nature, fertility, and Islam. The "sun" represents peace and creativity and its color the people's struggles.

KABARDINO-BALKARIA

The flag's colors evoke the blue sky, the white snow-capped mountains, and the green prairies of Kabardino-Balkaria. In the center is a stylized representation of the Elbrus Mountains.

KALMYKIA

The vibrant yellow is symbolic of the faith of the people of Kalmykia and also represents the sun warming their land. The blue circle signifies the eternal road to the sacred lotus in the center.

KARACHAY-CHERKESSIA

Blue symbolizes peace, kind motives, and quietness. Green represents nature, fertility, and wealth. Red is for the warmth and unity of the people. The mountains in the center recall the scenery of the republic.

KARELIA

The many lakes of Karelia are recalled by the central blue stripe, and its vast pine forests by green. The red stripe symbolizes warmth, unity, and continuing cooperation between the peoples of Karelia.

KHAKASSIA

The horizontal white, blue, and red stripes are taken from the Russian national flag. The vertical green stripe is for eternal life and is charged with an ancient Khakassian solar symbol.

KOMI

The three colors of the flag recall the republic's northerly location in blue, its forests in green, and its snows in white. They are also symbolic of such virtues as cleanliness, unity, and purity.

MARIY EL

The colors are adapted from the Russian national flag, with altered shades to make them distinctive. The name of the republic appears below the sun emblem.

MORDVINIA

The flag of Mordvinia was adopted in 1995, and has the same colors as the Russian flag. In the center is the sun emblem also found on the flags of Mariy El and Udmurtia.

NORTH
OSSETIA

White symbolizes spirituality and cleanliness of intentions. Yellow represents the region's farming. The red stripe recalls both the Aryan people and their militant spirit in pursuit of freedom.

TUVA

The original Tuvan flag adopted in 1918 was also blue, yellow, and white. Today, the colors are said to represent courage and strength in blue, prosperity in yellow, and purity in white.

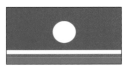

YAKUTIA

The flag recalls the blue sky and shining sun. Beneath is a white stripe recalling the snow. Red is for courage and constancy; green is for the forests of Yakutia.

TATARSTAN

The upper green stripe of the flag represents the majority Muslim Tatar population of Tatarstan. The lower red stripe is for the Russian minority. The white fimbriation represents the peace that unites them.

UDMURTIA

The eight-pointed solar sign in the center of the flag is said to guard the people from misfortune. The earth and stability are symbolized in black, morality and the cosmos in white, and life and the sun in red.

AZERBAIJAN

Ratio: *1:2*   Adopted: *February 5, 1991*   Usage: *National and Civil*

Blue is often associated with the Turkic people

Green is the traditional color of Islam

Red recalls European influence

Each point of the star represents a Turkic people

The colors represent the Azerbaijani motto to "Turkify, Islamize, and Europeanize"

ASIA

AZERBAIJAN HAS BEEN under consecutive Persian, Ottoman, and Russian influence. It was part of the USSR from 1920, until independence in 1991.

The flag dates back to the brief period of Azerbaijani independence between 1918–1920 and replaces the one used in the Soviet era. The white crescent and eight-pointed star were intentionally similar to the emblem on the Turkish flag, because Turkey has traditionally been an ally of the country. The eight points on the flag's star stand for the eight groups of Turkic-speaking peoples: the Azeris, Ottomans, Jagatais, Tatars, Kipchaks, Seljuks, and Turkomans.

THE NATIONAL ARMS
The coat of arms, adopted in 1993, is set on a round shield in the colors of the flag.

ARMS OF AZERBAIJAN

The flame at the star's center symbolizes a new era

The shield is in the color of the national flag; blue, red, and green

The star has eight points, each representing one of the eight Turkic peoples

The golden ear of corn reflects Azerbaijan's agriculture

ARMENIA

Ratio: *1:2*   Adopted: *August 24, 1990*   Usage: *National and Civil*

Red recalls
Armenian
blood spilled
during the
struggle for
independence

Blue is for
hope and the
Armenian
skies

Orange represents the blessings of hard work

ASIA

ARMENIA BECAME a Soviet republic in 1922. In 1991 it gained independence from the USSR and in 1995 held its first parliamentary elections.

Armenia was independent from 1920 to 1921, and the flag used today comes from this era. Its origin is in a design from the Armenian Institute in Venice of 1885, although this flag used the colors red-green-blue. After independence from Russia in 1991, the Soviet flag was replaced by the 1920 tricolor of red-blue-orange.

ARMS OF ARMENIA

In 1991, the arms of 1920 replaced the Soviet coat of arms. The four emblems within the shield each represent an Armenian royal dynasty. In the center is a stylized image of Mount Ararat. The shield is supported by an eagle and a lion, common symbols in Armenian heraldry.

ARMS OF ARMENIA

Mount Ararat, the
supposed resting place of
Noah's Ark, is in the
center of the arms

Four quarters of the
shield represent
former Armenian
royal dynasties

Below the shield lie a
broken leaf, a sheaf of
wheat, a pen, and a
sword

173

TURKEY

Ratio: *2:3*   Adopted: *June 5, 1936*   Usage: *National and Civil*

The star and crescent are both common symbols of the Islamic religion

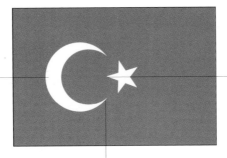

One star point touches the invisible line that joins the two horns of the crescent moon

The emblems are always placed slightly toward the hoist

FOLLOWING TURKEY'S defeat in World War I, Mustafa Kemal Atatürk deposed the Sultan in 1922 and declared the country a republic in 1923.

Turkey's flag dates from 1844, although similar red flags were used as early as the 17th century within the Ottoman Empire. From 1920 to 1923, when Turkey became a republic, all the emblems of the Sultan were abolished, and the flag became the main emblem.

THE CRESCENT AND STAR

Using the crescent and star emblems together is a relatively recent device, but the crescent on its own dates back to the Middle Ages. It is a symbol associated with Islam and also with Osman, the founder of the Ottoman Empire. The star first appeared on the flag in 1793. Initially it had eight points, but by the early 19th century it had the five points usually seen today. In 1936, the national flag and all the other flags used in Turkey today were fully defined and specified.

A PAN-ISLAMIC SYMBOL

The crescent and star has become an emblem of the Pan-Islamic movement sponsored by Turkey in the late 19th century, and these symbols are now widely used on the flags and national arms of Muslim countries.

Turkey does not have a coat of arms, but there are individual flags for the President and senior members of the Turkish navy. These also contain the traditional crescent and star.

GEORGIA

Ratio: *3:5*   Adopted: *November 14, 1990*   Usage: *National and Civil*

Black
represents
Georgia's
tragic past

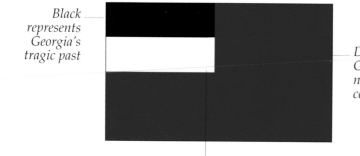
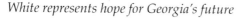

Deep red is
Georgia's
national
color

White represents hope for Georgia's future

ASIA

GEORGIA WAS ABSORBED into the Russian Empire in 1801 and became part of the Soviet Union in 1921. It regained independence in 1991.

The Georgian flag was chosen following a competition for a state flag in 1917 and was adopted by the country during its brief period of independence between 1918 and 1921.

THE SOVIET ERA
While part of the USSR, the current flag was suppressed and Georgia flew a variation of the Red Flag *(see page 6)*. This flag was adopted in 1951. It had a red field, with a thin blue stripe close to the top of the flag. In the canton it contained the traditional hammer, sickle, and star emblems. However, Georgia's flag was distinct from the flags of the other Soviet Socialist Republics, in

that the hammer, sickle, and star were in red, not gold. They were outlined by a blue disc, from which emanated 24 rays.

Following independence from the USSR in 1991, the 1918 flag was officially readopted, although with slightly modified dimensions.

THE SYMBOLISM OF THE COLORS
The field of the flag is deep wine red, the Georgian national color. When it was first adopted in 1918, it represented Georgia's bright past. Today it is also said to symbolize joy. The black and white stripes of the canton are said to symbolize Georgia's tragic past and hopeful future.

LEBANON

Ratio: *1:2*   Adopted: *December 7, 1943*   Usage: *National*

The white band symbolizes peace

The cedar tree represents holiness, eternity, and strength

The two red stripes are a symbol of self-sacrifice

ASIA

LEBANON BECAME INDEPENDENT in 1944, after 20 years as a French mandate. The country is currently rebuilding after 14 years of civil war.

The present Lebanese flag was adopted just prior to independence from France in 1943. It was designed to be a neutral flag, not allied to any one of Lebanon's religious groups. Red is thought to be for the color of the uniforms worn by the Lebanese Legion during World War I. Officially the red is said to represent the people of Lebanon's sacrifice during the struggle for independence, and white represents purity.

THE CEDAR OF LEBANON
Although the flag has existed only for half a century, the tree at the center of the flag – the Cedar of Lebanon – has been an emblem of the country since the time of King Solomon, almost 2000 years ago. Specifically, the cedar is the symbol of the country's Maronite Christian community. It first appeared on a flag in 1861 when the Lebanon was part of the Ottoman Empire. Soon after its collapse, the country became mandated to France and its flag was a French *Tricolore*, with the Cedar of Lebanon in the white band of the *Tricolore*. The cedar symbolizes happiness and prosperity for the country.

The present flag, with the cedar's foliage and trunk in green, has a variant in which the tree trunk is brown – although this is not officially recognized.

SYRIA

Ratio: *1:2*   Adopted: *March 29, 1980*   Usage: *National and Civil*

The two green stars originally represented Syria and Egypt, although they are now said to represent Syria and Iraq

An earlier version of the flag had three stars, in anticipation of a union incorporating Syria, Egypt, and Iraq

Red, white, black, and green are Pan-Arab colors

ASIA

SYRIA WAS CREATED after the dissolution of French colonial rule in 1946. From 1958–1961 it merged with Egypt to form the United Arab Republic.

In 1920, while still a French colony, Syria flew a green-white-green triband with a French *Tricolore* in the canton. At independence this was changed to a green, white, and black tricolor, with three red stars for its provinces across its center. Its current red, white, and black Pan-Arabic flag was adopted when Syria became part of the United Arab Republic but showing three stars. On leaving the union in 1961, Syria briefly reverted to its original flag, before readopting the Arab Liberation colors in 1963.

The arms of Syria depict the Hawk of Quraish. It is almost identical to the arms of Libya.

ARMS OF SYRIA

The shield is in the form of a national flag

The hawk was the emblem of the Quraish tribe to which the Prophet Muhammad belonged

The Arabic inscription reads "Arab Republic of Syria"

CYPRUS

Ratio: *3:5*   Adopted: *August 16, 1960*   Usage: *National and Civil*

The copper-
colored island
recalls the
origins of the
country's name

The two olive
branches
signify peace
between the
Turks and
Greeks

Neutral and peaceful symbols were
chosen to represent the country

ASIA

IN 1960, CYPRUS gained independence after almost 100 years of British rule. In 1974, the island was partitioned, following an invasion by Turkey.

Founded in 1193, the Kingdom of Cyprus experienced centuries of conflict. Cyprus was conquered by the Ottoman Empire in 1571, which increased Turkish settlement on the island. It then fell under British control in 1878. The flag, adopted at independence in 1960, deliberately chose peaceful and neutral symbols in an attempt to indicate harmony between the rival Greek and Turkish communities, an ideal that has not yet been realized.

In 1974, Turkish forces occupied the northern part of the island, forming the Turkish Republic of Northern Cyprus. The two parts of the island also fly the national flags of Greece and Turkey.

THE ISLE OF COPPER
The map of the island on the flag is supposed to be copper colored, to express the meaning of the island's name – the Isle of Copper – but it is usually shown as yellow. The two olive branches on the white field represent peace between the two ethnic groups.

THE NATIONAL EMBLEM
Cyprus's national emblem is a dove holding an olive branch in its beak. This is a symbol of peace and reconciliation arising from the biblical story of Noah and the Ark. The dove is also symbolic of Aphrodite, the Greek goddess whose legend originated from the island.

ISRAEL

Ratio: *8:11* Adopted: *October 28, 1948* Usage: *National*

The blue and white colors of the flag are said to be derived from the Jewish prayer shawl

The central emblem is the Star of David, which has a long association with the Jewish people

ASIA

ISRAEL WAS CREATED in 1947, following the UN Resolution (147) on Palestine. Until 1979 there were no official borders, only ceasefire lines.

The flag was designed for the Zionist movement by David Wolfsohn in 1891, over 50 years before the state of Israel was officially declared.

STAR OF DAVID
The central emblem in the form of a hexagram is known as the *Magen David* (Star of David), an emblem that had been used on Jewish flags for centuries before being adopted as the national flag of Israel. The blue and white colors are said to recall the colors of the *tallith* (Jewish prayer shawl). The blue is officially described as "Yale Blue." It is a lighter shade than used in other Israeli flags.

The merchant flag was adopted in 1948. There is also a naval ensign of similar design.

THE MERCHANT FLAG

The Star of David is slightly elongated on the merchant flag

Like other variant Israeli flags, the merchant flag is a darker shade of blue than the national flag

JORDAN

Ratio: *1:2*   Adopted: *April 16, 1928*   Usage: *National and Civil*

The seven-
pointed star
represents
the seven
verses of
Islamic
belief that
open the
Qur'an

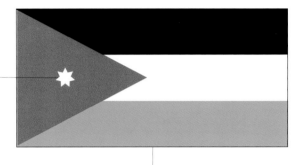

Red, black, green, and white are Pan-Arab colors

ASIA

ORIGINALLY CALLED TRANSJORDAN, as part of the Ottoman Empire, Jordan was officially renamed when independence was gained in 1946.

The colors of the Jordanian flag are those of the Pan-Arab flag. They were first used in 1917 to represent "pan-Arabianism," which sought independence from the Ottoman Empire. The star at the hoist was added in 1928, when Jordan gained nominal independence. It represents seven verses of Islamic belief.

ARMS OF JORDAN
The coat of arms is similar to that designed in 1339 for the King. The crest is a crown in his honor. The current inscription on the scroll reads "The King of the Hashemite Kingdom of Jordan, al-Husayn-bin-Talal bin-Abdulla, Beseeches the Almighty for Aid and Success."

ARMS OF JORDAN

The current coat of arms
is very similar to that
designed for King Hussein
in the 14th century

An Arabic inscription
asking for the
Almighty's aid

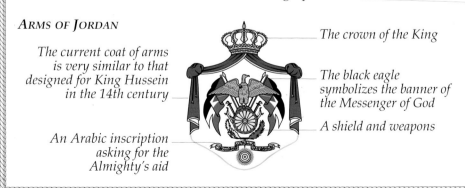

The crown of the King

The black eagle
symbolizes the banner of
the Messenger of God

A shield and weapons

SAUDI ARABIA

Ratio: 2:3   Adopted: 1973   Usage: National and Civil

A number of versions of the green flag have been used by the Wahabi sect since the 19th century

The shahada is the Muslim Statement of Faith

Green was thought to be a favorite color of the prophet Muhammad

ASIA

THE KINGDOM OF SAUDI ARABIA was unified under King Abd-al Aziz (ibn Sa'ud) in 1932. The Sa'ud family are the country's absolutist rulers.

The flag of Saudi Arabia symbolizes the Arab peoples of the desert. Used in various forms since the late 19th century, the green is favored by the Wahabi sect and is believed to be the favorite color of the prophet Muhammad.

THE SHAHADA.
In 1901, the *shahada*, the Muslim Statement of Faith, was added to the flag in white letters, making it one of only two national flags to contain an inscription.

By law it must be able to be read correctly – from right to left – on both sides of the flag. The sword is the symbolic sword of Abd-al-Aziz, who conquered part of Arabia in the early 20th century. It has appeared in different forms in the past, sometimes as two crossed swords.

THE SHAHADA

The inscription reads "There is no God but Allah and Muhammad is the Prophet of Allah"

This version of the sword was added in 1981

The sword represents that given to Abd-al-Aziz by his father

YEMEN

Ratio: 2:3 Adopted: *May 22, 1990* Usage: *National and Civil*

The flag adopted
for the united state
was based on the
common tricolor of
former flags of
North and South
Yemen

Red,
white,
and black
are Pan-
Arab
colors

ASIA

AFTER THREE centuries of rule by the Zaydi
Imams, Yemen split into two countries in 1962.
It reunited in 1990.

The first flag of the Yemen, used
while the Imams were in power, was
red with a white sword placed
horizontally in the center and five
white stars representing the five
duties of a devout Muslim. When
the two separate states were
established 1962, each adopted
its own flag.

SOUTH YEMEN

The flag of the People's Democratic
Republic of Yemen was modeled on
the Egyptian Pan-Arab flag. It was a
red, white, and black tricolor and it
bore a blue triangle, representing the
Yemeni people in the hoist, while a
red star represented the Socialist
ruling party.

NORTH YEMEN

The flag of the Yemen Arab Republic
was also modeled on the Egyptian
flag. It was a red, white, and black
tricolor, but it was simply charged
with a single, five-pointed green star
in a central white band, representing
Arab unity.

A UNIFIED FLAG

When the two countries were
unified, the stars and the triangle
were dropped, but the common
elements of their flags – the Pan-
Arab red, white, and black stripes –
were preserved for the new united
flag. The new flag's pattern suggests
a compromise between the officially
secular south and the Islamic north.

OMAN

Ratio: *1:2*   Adopted: *April 25, 1995*   Usage: *National and Civil*

The emblem of the ruling dynasty

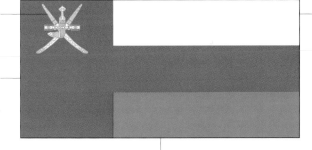

White is for the Imam of Oman and for peace

The red field is common in the flags of the Gulf states

Green represents the mountains and fertility

ASIA

IN 1970, THE PRESENT Sultan, Qaboos bin Said, overthrew his father and renamed the country as the Sultanate of Oman.

Until 1970, Oman used the plain red banner of the indigenous people, the Kharijite Muslims. In 1970, the Sultan introduced a complete new set of national flags. Bands of green and white were added to the fly, and the national emblem, the badge of the Albusaidi Dynasty, was placed in the canton. This depicts crossed swords over a *gambia*, a traditional curved dagger.

THE SYMBOLISM OF THE COLORS
White has been associated historically with the Imam, the religious leader of Oman and at times the political rival to the ruling Sultan. It also symbolizes peace. Green is traditionally associated with the *Jebel al Akhdar*, or "Green Mountains," which lie toward the north of the country. Red is a common color in Gulf state flags.

THE NATIONAL EMBLEM

The national emblem is said to date back to the middle of the 18th century

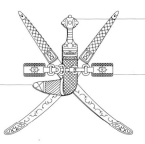

A curved dagger is fastened over a pair of crossed swords

An ornate horse-bit links the weapons

UNITED ARAB EMIRATES

Ratio: *1:2*   Adopted: *December 2, 1971*   Usage: *National and Civil*

Historically, the flags of the emirates were plain red

Green is for trees and fertility

White symbolizes neutrality

Black represents the oil wealth of the emirates

ASIA

THE UNITED ARAB EMIRATES is an amalgamation of seven emirates, formerly known as the Trucial States, that came together in 1971.

Following a General Treaty in 1820, the seven emirates that now form the United Arab Emirates came under British protection. Red and white flags were taken up by all except the Emirate of Fujairah, a nonsignatory to the treaty, which adopted a plain red flag. With minor alterations, the flags are still retained for local use. The first flag of the federation, adopted in 1968, was also red and white, but with a green star.

THE PAN-ARAB COLORS

On independence in 1971, a flag in the Pan-Arab colors – red, green, white, and black – was adopted to express Arab unity and nationalism. The red also recalls the color of the flags of the member states.

FLAG OF DUBAI

Like the other six emirates, Dubai retains its individual red and white flag

The flag colors remain constant, but the proportions have changed in recent decades

QATAR

Ratio: *11:28*   Adopted: *c. 1949*   Usage: *National and Civil*

"*Qatar maroon*" *derives from the action of sun on natural red dye*

The maroon coloring and proportions distinguish the flag from Bahrain's flag

ASIA

FORMERLY LINKED TO BAHRAIN, Qatar was in a treaty relationship with Britain from 1916 until 1971, when it gained full independence.

Qatar's flag was originally plain red, like the flag of Bahrain, to which it was once linked. The peoples of both countries are Kharijite Muslims, whose traditional banner was red. The flag evolved in its present form around the middle of the 19th century and was officially adopted when Qatar became independent from Britain in 1971.

zigzag, white interlock derives from a British request in the 1820s, that all friendly states around the Gulf add a white band to their flags, to distinguish them from pirate flags. During its earlier usage, before Qatar's independence, the flag also bore the name of the state in white lettering, and red diamonds were placed on the white band.

'QATAR MAROON'

The flag's maroon color is said to have come about from the action of the desert sun's heat on the red vegetable dyes formerly used for its flags. This color, now known as "Qatar maroon," was officially adopted in 1948. The nine-pointed,

THE EMBLEM OF QATAR

The circular badge of Qatar uses both the colors and serrated pattern of the flag around its edge. In the center is a local sailboat, passing an island. This is set between two crossed swords. It is inscribed with the name of the state in Arabic.

BAHRAIN

Ratio: *3:5*   Adopted: *2002*   Usage: *National and Civil*

The serrated edge was originally a straight line

Red and white are the traditional colors of the Gulf states

ASIA

BAHRAIN
Iran
Saudi Arabia
Qatar

DESPITE IRAN'S CLAIMS of sovereignty, Bahrain, an archipelago in the Gulf, has retained its independence gained from Great Britain in 1971.

Bahrain was under British protection from 1820 to 1971. By the terms of the General Maritime Treaty of 1820, all friendly states in the Gulf undertook to add white borders to their red flags, so that they would not be taken for pirate flags. The various states of the "Pirate Coast" then developed flags with differing white patterns on them. A plain vertical white strip was added to Bahrain's flag. In 1932 it achieved its modern form, when the line was serrated to distinguish the flag from that of Dubai.

The national arms was adopted in 1932. It is based on the colors and design of the national flag.

ARMS OF BAHRAIN

The coat of arms dates from 1932; it was designed by Sir Charles Belgrave, the sheik's political adviser

Until independence in 1971, there was an oriental crown above the shield

The shield contains the characteristic serrated division line, as on the national flag

KUWAIT

Ratio: *1:2*   Adopted: *September 7, 1961*   Usage: *National and Civil*

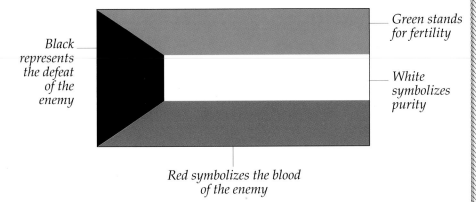

Black represents the defeat of the enemy

Green stands for fertility

White symbolizes purity

Red symbolizes the blood of the enemy

ASIA

THE STATE OF KUWAIT traces its independence to 1710, but it was under British rule from the late 18th century until 1961.

Before 1961, the flag of Kuwait, like those of other Gulf states, was red and white. The present flag is in the Pan-Arab colors, but each color is also significant in its own right. Black symbolizes the defeat of the enemy, while red is the color of blood on the Kuwaiti swords. White symbolizes purity, and green is for the fertile land. The idea for the flag's distinctive design – a horizontal tricolor with a black trapezium in the hoist – may have come from the flag used by Iraq until the late 1950s.

ARMS OF KUWAIT
The arms depicts a hawk containing an Arab *dhow* on stylized waves.

ARMS OF KUWAIT

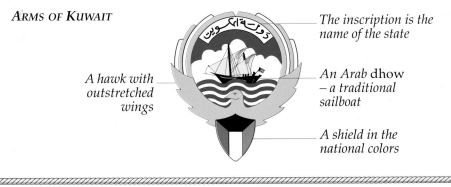

The inscription is the name of the state

A hawk with outstretched wings

An Arab dhow *– a traditional sailboat*

A shield in the national colors

IRAQ

Ratio: 2:3   Adopted: *January 14, 1991*   Usage: *National and Civil*

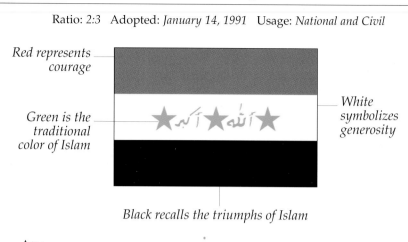

Red represents courage

White symbolizes generosity

Green is the traditional color of Islam

Black recalls the triumphs of Islam

ASIA

Turkey
Syria
IRAQ   Iran
Jordan
Saudi Arabia   Kuwait

ONCE PART of the Ottoman Empire, Iraq has been independent since 1932. The monarchy was overthrown and a republic proclaimed in 1958.

Since the flag of the Arab Revolt was first raised in 1917, Iraq's flag has contained the four Pan-Arab colors in various guises. The colors are said to represent the qualities of those who follow Islam. Red represents courage, white stands for generosity, black is for the triumphs of Islam, and green is for the religion itself. The present pattern of Iraq's flag dates from 1963 and is based on the Nasserite flag of Egypt. It was designed in anticipation of a political union with Egypt and Syria that never materialized.

THE NATIONAL ARMS
At the same time that the Nasserite flag was adopted, the golden Eagle of Saladin, another symbol of the United Arab Republic, was adopted as the national arms.

ISLAMIC VERSE

Three stars are for Iraq, Syria, and Egypt

The verse reads Allahu Akbar ("God is Great")

During the 1991 Gulf War, the Islamic phrase was added to the design by President Saddam Hussein

IRAN

Ratio: 4:7   Adopted: *July 29, 1980*   Usage: *National and Civil*

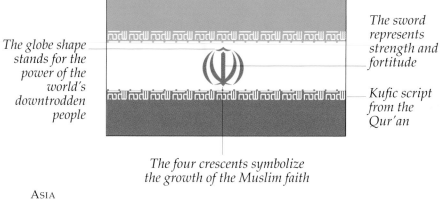

The sword represents strength and fortitude

The globe shape stands for the power of the world's downtrodden people

Kufic script from the Qur'an

The four crescents symbolize the growth of the Muslim faith

ASIA

IRAN WAS A monarchy until 1979, when the Ayatollah Khomeini deposed the Shah; an Islamic republic was formed in 1980.

The traditional green, white, and red of the Iranian flag date back to the 18th century, although there is no agreed explanation of the colors. The colors were arranged in horizontal stripes in 1906. In 1980 a new flag was introduced with the addition of emblems expressive of the Islamic Revolution.

A REVOLUTIONARY EMBLEM
The emblem in the center of the flag is a highly stylized composite of various elements representing different facets of Islamic life: Allah, the Book, the Sword, the five principles of Islam, balance, unity, neutrality, and the universal government of the downtrodden.

THE KUFIC SCRIPT
(stylized version)

A stylized version of Kufic script, used for the Qur'an

Along the edges of the green and red stripes appears the phrase Allahu Akbar *("God is Great")*

The script, repeated 22 times, is the date in the Islamic calendar on which Ayatollah Khomeini returned from exile in 1979

189

TURKMENISTAN

Ratio: *1:2*   Adopted: *February 19, 1997*   Usage: *National and Civil*

The wreath of olive leaves is identical to those on the United Nations flag and was added in 1997

Each star represents one of the five Turkmen regions

Green is a color revered in Turkmenistan

The ornamentation represents the five traditional carpet designs

ASIA

TURKMENISTAN WAS ORIGINALLY one of the 15 federated states of the USSR. It broke away and became an independent republic in 1991.

The original design of the flag was adopted on February 19, 1992, following a competition, and is based on national traditions. In the official interpretation, the five stars stand for the new regions established by the constitution of 1992. The carpet design contains five medallions, or *guls*, said to represent the traditional designs used by the tribes who produced the country's famous carpets. The wreath of olive leaves was added in 1997 to "immortalize the policy of neutrality" declared by Turkmenistan in 1995.

The coat of arms recalls the region's important agricultural products and famous horses.

ARMS OF TURKMENISTAN

The five guls from the national flag

Both cotton and wheat featured on the emblem of the former Soviet Republic of Turkmenistan

An akheltikin horse, famed in Turkmenistan

Cotton represents the country's most important agricultural product

UZBEKISTAN

Ratio: *1:2*   Adopted *November 18, 1991*   Usage: *National and Civil*

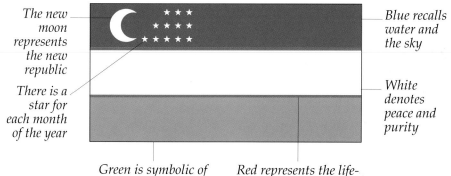

The new moon represents the new republic

There is a star for each month of the year

Blue recalls water and the sky

White denotes peace and purity

Green is symbolic of nature and fertility

Red represents the life-force in all people

ASIA

ONCE PART OF THE Mongol Empire, Uzbekistan fell to Russia in the late 19th century. It became independent from the USSR in 1991.

Uzbekistan was the first of the Central Asian republics to adopt its own non-Communist national flag, although the new design is based on that of the former Soviet Uzbekistan.

The blue stripe symbolizes water and the sky. It is also the color of the flag of Timur, who ruled an Uzbek empire in the 14th century. The white stripe is a sign of peace and purity. Green is a Muslim symbol of nature and fertility. Red is for the life force found in all people. The new moon suggests the birth of the new republic, while the 12 stars represent the months of the Islamic calendar.

The coat of arms, adopted in 1992, is similar to the previous arms.

ARMS OF UZBEKISTAN

The arms features a bird whose outstretched wings form a crescent framing a rising sun over a landscape of mountains and rivers

Cotton is Uzbekistan's chief cash crop

Islamic crescent and star

Wheat represents the country's staple food crop

The ribbon bears the name of the state

KAZAKHSTAN

Ratio: *1:2*   Adopted: *June 4, 1992*   Usage: *National and Civil*

The sky-blue field symbolizes the skies stretching over the many Kazakh people

A berkut, or steppe eagle, beneath a shining sun

The traditional national ornamentation is placed close to the hoist

ASIA

PART OF CENTRAL ASIA conquered by Russia in the 18th century, Kazakhstan was the last and largest republic to secede from the USSR.

Kazakhstan's post-Communist flag was adopted in 1992. Its sky-blue background recalls the endless skies over the Kazakh people. It also symbolizes well-being, tranquillity, peace, and unity. In the center of the flag, below a golden sun with 32 rays, soars a bird of the species known locally as the *berkut*, or steppe eagle. Together they represent love, freedom, and the aspirations of the Kazakh people. A pattern of what is described as national ornamentation forms a vertical stripe near the hoist.

The new coat of arms is also based around a radiant sun. It depicts traditional features of Kazakhstan.

ARMS OF KAZAKHSTAN

The sun's rays spread out like a yurt's *supporting structure*

The center of the arms recalls the upper part of a yurt, *the ancient felt tent of the Kazakh nomads*

Winged and horned horses represent historical traditions and beliefs

192

MONGOLIA

Ratio: *2:1*   Adopted: *1940*   Usage: *Civil and State*

The soyonbo device combines a number of Buddhist emblems

Originally the color of Communism, today red represents progress

Sky blue is the national color of Mongolia

ASIA

THIS REMOTE STATE has been under Communist rule since 1924. The former Communist Party was democratically reelected in 1997.

The current national flag replaced the Red flag of revolution in 1940. The red field is retained at the fly and hoist, although the color's original socialist connotations have given way to more general themes of progress and prosperity. The sky-blue panel represents the people of Mongolia and has come to express a growing nationalism, invoking the imperial days of Genghis Khan. Despite the state's atheist stance, the flag bears a 17th-century Buddhist emblem at hoist called the *soyonbo*. The *soyonbo* comprises various ideograms representing different elements from the Buddhist view of the world.

THE SOYONBO

The tongues of the flame stand for past, present, and future

Horizontal bars indicate that vigilance is required from the highest and lowest in society

The sun and moon represent ancestors of the Moguls

The vertical columns illustrate the Mongolian proverb: "Two friends are stronger than stone"

The fish stand for vigilance, because fish never sleep

KYRGYZSTAN

Ratio: *3:5*   Adopted: *March 3, 1992*   Usage: *National and Civil*

Red is
for Manas the
Noble, the
national hero

The sun's 40
rays stand for
the 40 tribes of
the Kyrgyz
nation

A stylized yurt, *the traditional home of
nomadic people*

ASIA

CONQUERED BY RUSSIA under the czars, in 1991 the Republic of Kyrgyzstan became the last of the Soviet Union Republics to declare sovereignty.

Independent since 1991, a post-Communist flag was not adopted until 1992. The flag's red background is supposed to be the flag color used by the national hero, Manas the Noble, who welded 40 tribes together to form the Kyrgyz nation.

In the center of the flag is a yellow sun with 40 rays, representing the tribes and the legendary 40 heroes of Manas. The sun's rays run clockwise on the obverse of the flag and counterclockwise on the reverse.

A TRADITIONAL *YURT*
At the sun's center is a stylized bird's-eye view of the roof, or *tunduk*, of a Kyrgyz *yurt*, the traditional tent used by the nomadic

people of the steppe. It symbolizes the unity of time and space, the origin of life, hearth and home, and the history of the nomads.

ARMS OF KYRGYZSTAN
Like the arms of its neighbor, Kazakhstan, the coat of arms of Kyrgyzstan is round and does not contain a traditional shield. In the center is a white eagle with spread wings. Behind this are snow-capped mountains, representing the mighty Tien Shan and a radiant, rising sun. This scene is bordered by wreaths of cotton and wheat, both major agricultural products in Kyrgyzstan. The name of the state is inscribed in Cyrillic script at the top.

TAJIKISTAN

Ratio: *1:2* Adopted: *November 24, 1992* Usage: *National and Civil*

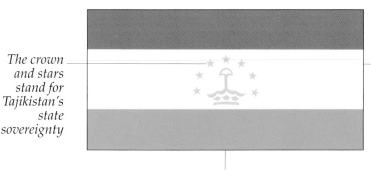

The crown and stars stand for Tajikistan's state sovereignty

White is the color of cotton, Tajikistan's main industry

Green represents farm produce

ASIA

A FORMER MEMBER of the USSR, Tajikistan proclaimed independence in 1991, but Russian and Communist influences remain strong.

In 1992, Tajikistan became the last of the former USSR republics to adopt a new flag. The red, white, and green stripes are the same as those chosen in 1953 for the flag of the Tadzhik Soviet Socialist Republic. Red is the color of the flag of the USSR; white is for cotton, Tajikistan's main export and green recalls other farm produce.

SYMBOLS OF THE NEW STATE
The center of the flag features a gold crown and an arc of seven stars. These symbols refer to the state sovereignty of Tajikistan, friendship between all nations, and the "unbreakable union of workers, peasants and the intellectual classes" of the republic.

ARMS OF TAJIKISTAN

The coat of arms from 1992 is dominated by a white lion with a yellow outline on a dark blue ground. The monutain beneath the lion recalls the country's many peaks

Crown and stars from the national flag

Wheat, a major crop, surrounds the arms

Red, white, and green ribbons

AFGHANISTAN

Ratio: *1:2* Adopted: *2002* Usage: *National*

Black recalls previous flags used in Afghanistan

Green represents Islam

The new arms of Afghanistan

Asia

THE TALIBAN REGIME, which had ruled Afghanistan from 1996, was ousted by US coalition forces in 2001. A transitional government is now in place.

The Transitional Administration in Afghanistan adopted a new national flag to replace the green, white and black flag of the Taliban government. The new design echoes the colours of the 1964 Constitution flag, with some minor changes.

A revised coat of arms has been added at the centre of the flag. Modifications to the old arms (shown below) have made it less war-like (the crossed swords have been removed) and more secular.

The black stripe recalls flags used by Afghanistan in the past and green is a symbol of the Islamic faith, prosperity and victory over imperialism.

EMBLEM OF TALIBAN AFGHANISTAN 1996–2002

A minabar *or pulpit*

The Arabic inscription reads,"There is no God but Allah and Muhammad is the Prophet of Allah"

The mosque contains a mihrab – *a niche in the mosque wall indicating the direction of Mecca*

1371 (AD 1992) is the date in Muslim calendar when mujahideen *achieved victory*

PAKISTAN

Ratio: *2:3*   Adopted: *August 14, 1947*   Usage: *National*

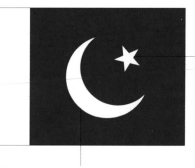

The white strip represents non-Muslim and other minority groups in Pakistan

Star symbolizes light and knowledge

The crescent represents progress

ASIA

ONCE A PART OF British India, Pakistan was created in 1947 as an independent Muslim state. Today, it is divided into four provinces.

The flag was designed by Muhammad Ali Jinnah, founder of the nation. It is associated with the flag used by the All-India Muslim League as an emblem of its aim of achieving an independent Muslim state. Their flag was green, with a central white star and crescent. At independence, a white stripe was added at the hoist to represent the state's minorities.

THE SYMBOLISM OF THE COLORS
The green and white together stand for peace and prosperity. The crescent symbolizes progress, and the star represents light and knowledge.

The flag of the President is similar to the national flag. The emblems are in gold and are enclosed within a wreath of laurel. Beneath is the name of the state in Urdu.

THE PRESIDENT'S FLAG

The field of the President's flag is green and white, like the national flag

The crescent and star are symbols of Islam

The name of the state is written in Urdu

NEPAL

Ratio: *4:3 (plus border)*   Adopted: *December 16, 1962*   Usage: *National and Civil*

The blue border denotes peace

The crescent moon represents the royal house

Red is the color of the rhododendron, Nepal's national flower

The sun represents the Rana family

ASIA

FROM 1960 NEPAL WAS RULED by an absolute monarchy. This regime ended in 1991 when the first multiparty elections were held.

The flag of Nepal is the only national flag that is not rectangular or square. Originally, two separate triangular pennants were flown one above the other; these were then joined to form a single flag. Its crimson red is the color of the rhododendron; the country's national flower. Red is also the sign of victory in war. The blue border is the color of peace.

THE SUN AND THE MOON

Until 1962, the flag's emblems, the sun and the crescent moon, had human faces. They were removed to modernize the flag. The faces remain on the sun and moon on the Royal Standard. The crescent represents the royal house, and the sun denotes the Rana family, who were hereditary prime ministers until 1961.

THE ROYAL STANDARD

The Royal Standard shows a rampant lion holding a lance with a flag

The sun and moon have faces, as did those on the national flag until 1962

BHUTAN

Ratio: 2:3   Adopted: c. 1965   Usage: National and Civil

Saffron yellow denotes the authority of the King

The Thunder Dragon

White represents purity and loyalty

Orange represents the Drukpa monasteries and religious practices

ASIA

BHUTAN IS A Buddhist state where power is shared by the king and government. The country's name in the local dialect means Land of the Dragon.

In Bhutan, thunder is believed to be the voices of dragons roaring. In about 1200, a monastery was set up called the *Druk* (the Thunder Dragon), with a sect, called the Drukpas, named after it. The name and the emblem of the dragon have been associated with Bhutan ever since. The dragon on the flag is white to symbolize purity.

TEMPORAL AND SPIRITUAL POWER
The two colors of the flag, divided diagonally, represent spiritual and temporal power within Bhutan. The orange part of the flag represents the Drukpa monasteries and Buddhist religious practice, while the saffron yellow field denotes the secular authority of the royal dynasty of the Wangchuks.

EMBLEM OF BHUTAN

The dragon symbolizes Druk, *the Tibetan name for the Kingdom of Bhutan*

Jewels clasped in the dragon's claws symbolize wealth

The snarling mouth expresses the strength of the male and female deities protecting the country

INDIA

Ratio: *2:3*   Adopted: *July 22, 1947*   Usage: *National*

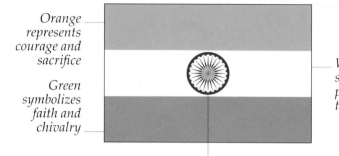

Orange
represents
courage and
sacrifice

Green
symbolizes
faith and
chivalry

White
symbolizes
peace and
truth

The Chakra, *or Buddhist spinning wheel*

ASIA

UNDER BRITISH RULE from 1763, the Indian subcontinent divided into Pakistan and India in 1947 upon independence.

The national flag, adopted in 1947, is based on the flag of the Indian National Congress, which was established in 1885 to press for independence. The flag's orange color symbolizes courage and sacrifice, white stands for peace and truth, green is for faith and chivalry, and blue represents the color of the sky and the ocean.

THE *CHAKRA*
The central motif is a *Chakra*, or Buddhist spinning wheel. The 24 spokes of the wheel correspond with the 24 hours of the day, implying that there is life in movement and death in stagnation.
   The naval ensign is based on that of Britain, with the Cross of St. George over all in the center.

INDIAN NAVAL ENSIGN

The national flag is
placed in the canton

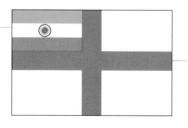

The naval ensign
contains the red Cross
of St. George

MALDIVES

Ratio: 2:3   Adopted: *July 26, 1965*   Usage: *National and Civil*

The panel of Islamic green symbolizes peace and prosperity

Red was the original color of the Maldives flag

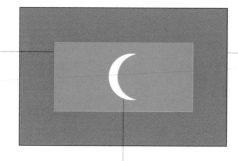

The crescent represents Islam

ASIA

THE ARCHIPELAGO of small islands that forms the Maldives was once a British Protectorate. The Maldives became fully independent in 1965.

Until the beginning of the 20th century the flag of the Maldives was plain red, reflecting the culture of the Arab traders from the Persian Gulf who operated among the islands. This flag remained in use after the British Protectorate was set up in 1887. The flag later acquired a white crescent facing the hoist – another sign of Islamic influence.

A NEW DESIGN
The flag was redesigned in 1948 after the independence of Ceylon (now Sri Lanka) of which the islands had been a dependency. The crescent was turned around and placed on an Islamic green panel. A pattern of black and white diagonal stripes was added along the hoist. This was dropped after independence from Britain in 1965. A modern interpretation of the colors suggests that red symbolizes the blood shed in the struggle for independence, while green stands for peace and progress.

THE NATIONAL ARMS
The coat of arms of the Maldives contains the Islamic crescent and star emblem beneath a date palm. Below the crescent is a scroll with the inscription, in Dihevi, "State of a Thousand Islands," which recalls the many islands which make up the Maldives. The crescent is flanked by two national flags.

SRI LANKA

Ratio: *1:2*   Adopted: *December 17, 1978*   Usage: *National and Civil*

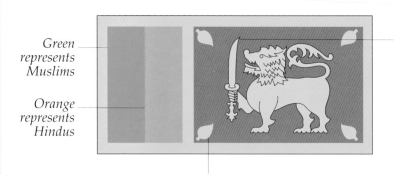

Green represents Muslims

Orange represents Hindus

The sword is a symbol of authority

The four pipul *leaves are Buddhist symbols*

ASIA

India

SRI LANKA

THE ISLAND OF CEYLON was a British colony until independence in 1948. It became a republic under the name Sri Lanka in 1972.

The original flag of Sri Lanka featured just the lion and sword on a red field, recalling that the Sinhalese word for lion – *Sinhala* – is the basis of the island's name. The flag's yellow border symbolized the protection of the nation by Buddhism.

The flag was derived from the flag of the Sinhalese kingdom of Kandy. It proved unpopular with minority groups, so vertical bands of green, for Muslims, and orange, for the Hindu Tamils, were added in 1951.

When the country's name changed from Ceylon to Sri Lanka in 1972, four leaves were added. They denote the tree under which Siddhartha sat when he received enlightenment and became the Buddha. This version of the flag was in official use from 1978.

FLAG OF KANDY

The Lion Flag was the national flag of Ceylon prior to 1815 when it became a British colony

The finials are derived from the spire on top of a Buddhist temple

BANGLADESH

Ratio: 3:5   Adopted: *January 25, 1972*   Usage: *National*

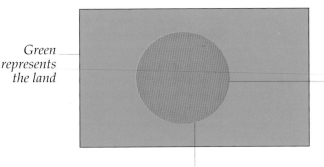

Green
represents
the land

The red disk
symbolizes the
struggle for
independence

*The red circle is set slightly
toward the hoist*

ASIA

BANGLADESH WAS FORMERLY the eastern province of Pakistan. After a civil war with Pakistan, it became a separate country in 1971.

The flag was originally adopted in March 1971 when the country gained independence, at which time it had a yellow silhouette map of the country in the red disk. This flag was used throughout the struggle for independence, but when the state was formally established in 1971 the outline map was omitted from the new national flag.

ARMS OF BANGLADESH
The coat of arms was adopted in 1972 and consists of the national flower, a water lily, known locally as the *shapla*, growing from stylized waves. Around it are ears of rice, a sprig of jute, and four golden stars. The arms appears in the center of the President's flag, set on a deep purple field.

THE PRESIDENT'S FLAG

Wreath of rice

A shapla *(winter lily)*
on stylized waves

The name of the state
in Bangla

A sprig of jute, with
four golden stars
representing
nationalism, socialism,
democracy, and
secularism

MYANMAR (BURMA)

Ratio: 2:3   Adopted: *January 4, 1974*   Usage: *National and Civil*

The new socialist-style emblem was added in 1974

Red symbolizes courage

Blue represents peace

White represents purity

ASIA

In 1886, MYANMAR became a province of British India. It separated from India in 1937 and gained independence from British colonial control in 1948.

The flag originated in the Burman Resistance, which adopted a red flag with a white star when fighting the occupying Japanese forces during World War II. Upon independence, the star was modified to a blue canton with five small stars surrounding one large one, symbolizing the uniting of the country's diverse peoples. Red stands for the courage of the people, blue is for peace, and white is for purity.

The emblem was changed in 1974 to represent the new socialist ideology in the country. The five stars were changed to 14, encircling a cogwheel for industry, and a rice plant for agriculture.

EMBLEM OF MYANMAR

On the new socialist emblem, the rice stands for agriculture, while the cogwheel represents industry

14 stars represent the unity and equality between the 14 member states of the Union

THAILAND

Ratio: 2:3   Adopted: *September 28, 1917*   Usage: *National and Civil*

Red symbolizes life blood

White stands for the purity of the Buddhist faith

The blue and white stripes were added during World War I

Blue represents the monarchy

FORMERLY KNOWN AS the Kingdom of Siam, Thailand is the only Southeast Asian nation never to have been colonized.

Thailand is also known as the Land of the White Elephant, and this emblem appeared on its plain red flag in the 19th century. During World War I, horizontal white stripes were added above and below the elephant.

In 1917 the elephant was abandoned, and a blue stripe was added to the middle of the flag in order to express solidarity with the Allies, whose flags were mostly red, white, and blue. This flag is known as the *Trairanga* (tricolor).

The Royal Arms of Thailand was introduced in 1910. It features the *garuda*, a bird-man in Hindu mythology.

ARMS OF THAILAND

The **garuda** *of Hindu mythology is the enemy of all things poisonous*

The red **garuda** *is placed on a field of royal yellow for the Royal Standard*

LAOS

Ratio: *2:3*   Adopted: *December 2, 1975*   Usage: *National and Civil*

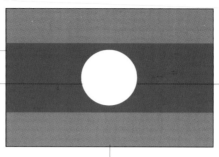

Blue represents wealth

The white disk on a blue stripe represents the full moon over the Mekong River

The white disk symbolizes unity under Communism

Red symbolizes the blood shed during the struggle for freedom

ASIA

A FRENCH PROTECTORATE from the end of the 19th century, Laos gained full independence in 1953. It has been under Communist rule since 1975.

The national flag of Laos was adopted in 1975, when the country became a people's republic. It is one of the few Communist flags that does not use the five-pointed star as an emblem. This flag replaced the original flag of Laos, which was red, with a triple-headed white elephant on a pedestal beneath a parasol. This expressed the ancient name of the country, "Land of a Million Elephants," and dated from the 19th century.

A FLAG FOR THE REPUBLIC

From 1953 onward the royal government waged war with the Pathet Lao, whose flag was blue with a white disk and red borders at the top and bottom. From 1973–1975, the Pathet Lao formed part of the government coalition, before assuming power directly and prompting the abdication of the king. Their flag was then adopted as the national flag.

In the center is a white disk symbolizing the unity of the people under the leadership of the Lao People's Revolutionary Party and the country's bright future. The red stripes stand for the blood shed by the people in their struggle for freedom, and the blue symbolizes their prosperity.

The white disk on a blue background is also said to represent a full moon against the Mekong River.

CAMBODIA

Ratio: 2:3   Adopted: *June 29, 1993*   Usage: *National and Civil*

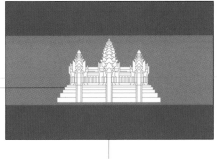

The famous temple of Angkor Wat has appeared in various forms on Cambodia's flag

Red and blue are traditional colors

CAMBODIA WAS A **French Protectorate until 1949** when it became nominally independent once more. Full independence was achieved in 1953.

The flag used today is the same as that established in 1948, although since then five other designs have been used. These have almost all made use of the image of the temple of Angkor Wat in one form or another. This famous temple site, which dates from the 12th century, was built by the Mahidharapura monarchs. It has five towers, but these were not always all depicted in the stylized version used on flags. The temple also appears on the arms. The monarchy was restored in September 1993, the 1948 flag having been readopted in June of that year.

ARMS OF CAMBODIA

The glowing sun represents national rebirth

Angkor Wat is a symbol of the nation and its greatness

The inscription is the name of the country

VIETNAM

Ratio: *2:3*   Adopted: *November 30, 1955*   Usage: *National and Civil*

The gold five-pointed star is for the unity of five groups of workers in building socialism

Red symbolizes revolution and bloodshed

ASIA

IN 1954 VIETNAM was divided into North and South. In 1976, the North finally achieved its aim of reunification under Communism.

Vietnam's national flag was adopted in 1976 at the end of the Vietnam War when North and South Vietnam were reunited under the new name of the Socialist Republic of Vietnam. This flag had been used by Communist North Vietnam since 1955, a year after partition.

It is basically the same as the flag used by the national resistance movement, led by Ho Chi Minh, in its struggle against the occupying Japanese forces during World War I.

SYMBOLISM OF THE COLORS
The red color of the field stands for the revolution and for the blood shed by the Vietnamese people. The five-pointed yellow star represents the unity of workers, peasants, intellectuals, youths, and soldiers in the building of socialism.

ARMS OF VIETNAM
The national coat of arms, which was also readopted in 1976, had been used by North Vietnam since 1956. It depicts a cogwheel, symbolic of industry, and the yellow five-pointed star of socialism, enclosed by a garland of rice – the country's main agricultural product. The name of the country is inscribed on a scroll at the base of the emblem. The symbols on both the arms and the flag were inspired by the Chinese flag.

MALAYSIA

Ratio: *1:2*   Adopted: *September 16, 1963*   Usage: *National and Civil*

The blue canton represents unity of the Malaysian people

The 14 red and white stripes for the 14 states of the Federation

The crescent and star of Islam

ASIA

Thailand
Brunei
MALAYSIA
Indonesia

MALAYA BECAME independent of Britain in 1957. In 1963, the Federation of Malaysia was formed, although Singapore seceded in 1965.

The first flag of independent Malaya was based on the Stars and Stripes of the United States, combined with Islamic symbolism. It had 11 red and white stripes and a blue canton, like the US flag, with a gold crescent and an eleven-pointed star, traditionally associated with Islam. Both the number of stripes and points on the star denoted the 11 states of the Federation.

THREE NEW STATES
In 1963 three new states – Singapore, Sabah, and Sarawak – joined the Federation to form Malaysia. To reflect this the flag was amended to 14 red and white stripes representing the 14 states. When Singapore seceded in 1965, the flag remained unaltered. The fourteenth stripe is now said to stand for the federal district of Kuala Lumpur.

THE SYMBOLISM OF THE COLORS
The blue canton represents the unity of the Malaysian people. The crescent is for Islam, the dominant religion. The 14 points of the star are for unity among the states of the country. Yellow is the traditional color of the rulers of the Malay states. Red and white are also traditional colors in Southeast Asia.

The national motto appears on a scroll in the coat of arms. It is repeated in both Jawi and Roman script and means "Unity is Strength."

Malaysia – State flags

THE FLAGS OF THE MALAYSIAN states were mostly derived from those of the 19th century and were originally flags of the princes or sultans.

 JOHORE

The blue field represents the government. The red canton is for the *Hulubalang* warrior caste, who defend the state. The crescent and star represent the ruler.

 KEDAH

Red is the traditional color of Kedah. The sheaves of yellow padi, or rice, are for prosperity. The green crescent signifies Islam and the yellow shield is for sovereignty.

 KELENTAN

The red field is symbolic of the loyalty and sincerity of the people, while the white emblem represents the ruler. Kelentan has 36 royal and official flags.

 KUALA LUMPUR

Blue is for the unity of the population of Kuala Lumpur; red for courage and vigor; white is for purity, cleanliness and beauty; yellow for sovereignty and prosperity.

 LABUAN

The colors are those of the national flag and they have the same symbolism; white recalls the purity of Buddhism, and red represents the lifeblood of the people.

 MELAKA

The colors and pattern are taken from the national flag. Unlike the Malaysian flag, the flag of Melaka has only one stripe of red and one of white, and a five-pointed star.

 NEGERI SEMBILAN

This flag reflects the hierarchy of power in Malaysia. The yellow field symbolizes the ruler, the black triangle the district rulers, and the red triangle the people.

 PAHANG

White is for the ruler, because it can change to any other color, reflecting how a ruler can be influenced by popular opinion. Black represents the people, standing firm.

PERAK

The three stripes represent different levels of the royal family. The Sultan is evoked by white, the Raja Muda by yellow, and the Raja di-Hilir by black. The latter two are junior members of the ruling family.

PERLIS

Yellow represents the ruler, and blue represents the people. The colors are arranged as two equal horizontal stripes to signify the close co-operation that should exist between the ruler and his subjects.

PINANG

Light blue represents the blue seas around the island of Pinang. White is for the peace and serenity of the state and yellow for its prosperity. The tree is the Pinang palm, after which the state is named.

SABAH

The zircon blue (top stripe) is for tranquillity, white for purity and justice, red for courage, ice-blue (canton) for unity and prosperity, and royal blue for strength. The mountain is Kinabalu.

SARAWAK

Yellow is the traditional color of Borneo, where the state lies. Red and black are from the flag of the former Raja of Sarawak. The star has nine points for the nine districts of the state.

SELANGOR

The yellow and red quarters are symbolic of flesh and blood, the combination necessary for life. The crescent and star in the canton represent Islam, the dominant religion of the state.

TERENGGANU

The white background stands for the Sultan. It envelopes the black field, symbolizing the people. This reflects how the Sultan provides protection around his subjects.

INDONESIA

Ratio: 2:3   Adopted: *August 17, 1945*   Usage: *National and Civil*

Red represents the body

White symbolizes the soul

The flag is based on the banner of the 13th-century Indonesian Empire

ASIA

A FORMER DUTCH COLONY, Indonesia gained independence in 1949. Western New Guinea (Irian Jaya) was ceded to Indonesia in 1963.

The flag is based on the banner of the 13th-century Empire of Majahapit, red and white being the holy colors of Indonesia at that time. These colors were revived in the 20th century as an expression of nationalism against the Dutch. The first red and white flag flew in Java in 1928 and was adopted as the national flag of the republic in 1945 when the country declared its independence. The red stripe is symbolic of physical life, while white represents spiritual life. Together they stand for the complete human being, body and soul. Red and white are also traditional colors of the Southeast Asian nations.

ARMS OF INDONESIA

The arms show a shield supported by a mythical bird, the garuda. The 17 wing-feathers and 8 tail-feathers refer to the day and month (August 17) on which independence was declared in 1945

The shield depicts a buffalo head, a banyan tree, and sheaves of rice and cotton

The yellow star represents religious belief

The national motto means "Unity in Diversity"

EAST TIMOR

Ratio: 2:3   Adopted: *Pending confirmation*   Usage: *National and Civil*

Black represents
the oppression
of the past

Red stands for
the struggle
for national
liberation

The white star
symbolizes hope

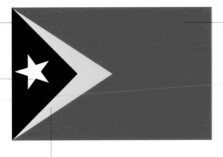

Yellow represents the
wealth of the country

ASIA

East Timor voted for independence from
Indonesia in 1999. A UN administration was in
place until official independence on May 20, 2002.

At midnight on May 19, 2002, the
UN flag was removed from outside
the government offices in Dili,
the capital. The new country, now
officially recognized as a national
state, has its own parliament, its
own president, and its own flag.

NEW STATE, OLD FLAG
The flag illustrated above is actually
the flag designed by the Fretilin party
for the "Democratic Republic of
Timor" in 1975, following the
transition from Portuguese colony to
independence. However, the infant
nation's subsequent invasion and
occupation by Indonesia led to the
adoption of that country's flag for the
last quarter of the twentieth century.

SYMBOLISM OF THE FLAG
The black triangle represents the
darkness of four centuries of colonial
oppression under the Portuguese.
The golden-yellow arrowhead recalls
the long struggle for independence,
as well as the hope of the country's
future prosperity. The red field
reflects the blood shed by the
Timorese people on their journey
towards autonomy – a symbol which
has taken on greater poignancy since
the referendum for independence
and the massacre of almost a million
East Timorese by pro-Indonesian
militias in 1999. The white of the star
symbolizes peace, whilst the star
itself represents the guiding light
which gives hope for the future.

SINGAPORE

Ratio: 2:3   Adopted: *December 3, 1959*   Usage: *National and Civil*

The crescent is for the new nation

The five stars symbolize ideals of democracy, peace progress, justice and equality

Red stands for universal brotherhood and equality

White represents the purity and virtue of the Singaporean people

ASIA

GRANTED SELF-GOVERNMENT by Britain in 1959, Singapore became part of the Federation of Malaysia in 1963 and fully independent in 1965.

The flag dates from when Singapore became a self-governing British colony in 1959. It was preserved when Singapore joined the Malaysian Federation and adopted as the national flag when Singapore became fully independent in 1965.

The colors of red and white are those of the Malay people. Red is supposed to represent universal brotherhood and equality, while white symbolizes purity and virtue. The white crescent signifies the new nation of Singapore, while the five stars next to it represent the ideals of democracy, peace, progress, justice, and equality.

The President's flag is a plain red field with the crescent and star emblem in the center.

THE PRESIDENT'S FLAG

The President's flag simply enlarges and centers the crescent and stars motif from the national flag

Red and white represents the Malay people

BRUNEI

Ratio: *1:2* Adopted: *September 29, 1959* Usage: *National and Civil*

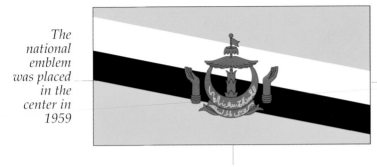

The national emblem was placed in the center in 1959

Black and white stripes represent Brunei's chief ministers

Yellow represents the Sultan of Brunei

ASIA

BRUNEI BECAME A British Protectorate in 1888. It gained full independence in 1984, and is now an absolute monarchy under its Sultan.

A similar version of this flag, without the coat of arms, was first used in 1906. The flag's main color, yellow, is associated with the Sultan, while the black and white stripes that cut across it are the colors of the Brunei's two chief ministers. The coat of arms in the center of the flag was added in 1959.

THE NATIONAL ARMS
The coat of arms bears testament to Brunei's Muslim traditions with the crescent, a traditional symbol of Islam, at its center. The Arabic motto on the crescent translates as, "Always render service by God's guidance," below it, a scroll bears the inscription *Brunei Darussalam* (City of Peace).

ARMS OF BRUNEI

The crescent is symbolic of the Islamic faith

The central mast is a symbol of the state

he flag and umbrella are symbols of royalty

The upturned hands signify the benevolence of the government

The inscription is the country's official title Brunei Darussalam

PHILIPPINES

Ratio: *1:2* Adopted: *May 19, 1898* Usage: *National and Civil*

The white
triangle
symbolizes
purity and
peace

Blue
represents
patriotism

Red
symbolizes
bravery

*The sun and stars represent the three main areas
of the country – Luzon, the Visayas, and Mindanao*

ASIA

THE PHILIPPINES was a Spanish colony until 1898, when it was ceded to the United States. It gained its independence in 1946.

The flag was first used by Filipino nationalists in exile while the Spanish still controlled the islands. When they were ceded to the USA, the Philippines became far more autonomous, and the flag was flown freely from 1898. It was banned by the Americans from 1907–1919, and the Stars and Stripes was then flown exclusively on the islands.

The sun and stars are Masonic in origin. The eight rays of the sun are for the eight provinces that revolted against the Spanish. The three stars represent the country's three main geographical areas. White stands for purity and peace; red for bravery, and blue for patriotism. When used in war, the red stripe is flown at the top of the flag, representing courage.

THE PRESIDENT'S FLAG

The sun is taken from
the national flag

The three stars and a
golden sealion were
adapted from the arms
of Manila

A ring of 52
white stars

TAIWAN

Ratio: *2:3*   Adopted: *October 28, 1928*   Usage: *National*

A blue flag with a white sun was the party flag of the Kuomingtang

The flag is said to represent a white sun in a blue sky over red land

Each ray represents two hours of a day

Red recalls the Han Chinese, the dominant race in China

ASIA

TAIWAN WAS formerly part of China. It became a separate state in 1949 under the Nationalist party, which was expelled from government in Beijing.

The flag adopted for Taiwan or Formosa, as it was known, had been the national flag of China. It was used from 1928–1949 when the Kuomingtang, the Chinese Nationalist party was in power.

The red field represents China; the blue canton and white sun was the party flag of the Kuomingtang. The 12 rays of sunshine symbolize

unending progress, each ray representing two hours of the day.

THE TAIPEI OLYMPIC FLAG
This flag was adopted by Taiwan specifically for use at the Olympic Games, where its national flag was not accepted. It combines red, white and blue; the national colors of Taiwan and the Olympic emblem.

THE TAIPEI OLYMPIC FLAG

The sun symbol is taken from the national flag

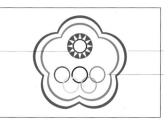

Blue, red, and white are the national colors

The emblem of connected rings shows that it is an Olympic flag

CHINA

Ratio: 2:3   Adopted: *October 1, 1949*   Usage: *National and Civil*

The large star
represents
communism

The four smaller
stars represent
the social classes
of the Chinese
people

The red field
symbolizes
communist
revolution and
is also the
traditional color
for the Chinese
people

*The use of five stars reflects the
importance of the number five in
Chinese philosophy*

ASIA

CHINA HAS THE WORLD'S oldest continuous
civilization. The communist Chinese People's
Republic was established in 1949.

China's first national flag originated
in 1872. It was yellow with a blue
dragon, representing the Manchu
(Qing) Dynasty, which ruled China
for many years. The revolt of 1911
saw the changing of the flag to five
different colored stripes. Soviet
republics were established in the
1920s, each of which was
represented by a red flag referring to
the Soviet fatherland. The present
flag dates from 1949, when the
People's Republic was formed.

The large star represents
Communism. The red field signifies
revolution and echoes the ancient
Han Dynasty of 206 BC. The four
stars represent the four social classes:
peasants, workers, petty bourgeoisie,
and patriotic capitalists.

*FLAG OF HONG KONG
(XIANGGANG) IN 1997*

*FLAG OF MACAO IN
1999*

NORTH KOREA

Ratio: *1:2*   Adopted: *September 9, 1948*   Usage: *National and Civil*

Two blue stripes stand for sovereignty, peace and friendship

The white stripes symbolize purity

Red represents Communist revolution

The star is a symbol of communism

ASIA

THE KINGDOM OF KOREA was annexed by Japan in 1910. In 1948, the peninsula was partitioned into a Communist north and a Democratic south.

The flag was adopted in 1948, when North Korea became an independent Communist state. The traditional Korean flag was red, white, and blue. The regime retained these colors – with more prominence given to the red – and added a red star on a white disk. The disk recalls the Chinese yin-yang symbol, which is found on the flag of South Korea, and represents the opposing principles of nature. The red stripe expresses revolutionary traditions; while the red star is for Communism.

The prominent theme of the Soviet-style coat of arms is industrialization, depicted with an electricity pylon and a large dam.

ARMS OF NORTH KOREA

The star of communism

A hydroelectric power station within a wreath of rice ears

Industrial elements feature heavily on the arms of Korea and include a large dam and electricity pylon

The inscription on the scroll is the country's official name – The Democratic People's Republic of Korea

SOUTH KOREA

Ratio: *2:3*   Adopted: *September 8, 1948*   Usage: *National and Civil*

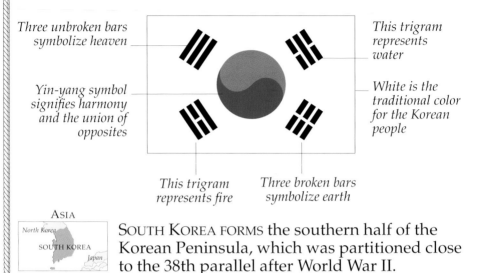

Three unbroken bars symbolize heaven

Yin-yang symbol signifies harmony and the union of opposites

This trigram represents water

White is the traditional color for the Korean people

This trigram represents fire

Three broken bars symbolize earth

ASIA

North Korea
SOUTH KOREA
Japan

SOUTH KOREA FORMS the southern half of the Korean Peninsula, which was partitioned close to the 38th parallel after World War II.

The flag used by the Kingdom of Korea before 1910 featured the traditional colors: of red, white, and blue. When South Korea separated from the north in 1948, the original flag was retained, but a few alterations were made.

A NEW SOUTH KOREAN FLAG
At the flag's center is a disc containing an S-shaped line, the upper half being red, the lower half blue. This is derived from the Eastern yin-yang symbol, which represents the harmony of opposites in nature — good and evil, male and female. When North and South Korea separated, the shape of the yin-yang was stylized in

the form of a Japanese *mon*. These are simplified versions of everyday objects, shown in symmetrical and regular forms. Yang is represented by red and yin by blue.

The other alteration to the original flag in 1948 was to the trigrams (*kwae*) surrounding the yin-yang, which were reduced from eight to four. They are the basic trigrams from the *I-Ching*, a divination system widespread in the East. On the South Korean flag they symbolize the four polarities; heaven (upper hoist), water (upper fly), fire (lower hoist), and earth (lower fly). The white field of the flag represents peace and the white clothing traditionally worn by the Korean people.

JAPAN

Ratio: 7:10   Adopted: January 27, 1870   Usage: National and Civil

The white field expresses honesty and purity

The red disk is named Hinomaru, *or disk of the sun*

The sun symbol has been an element in Japan's flag's for thousands of years

ASIA

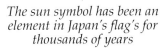

ISOLATED FROM the world for centuries, Japan began to modernize in the 19th century. After defeat in World War II, it became a democracy.

Japan is known as "The Land of the Rising Sun." The Emperor of Japan and his predecessors descend from the House of Yamato, which united the country in AD 200 and they claim to be direct descendants of the sun goddess, Amaterasu Omikami.

The current flag was officially established as the national flag of Japan in 1870.

THE *HINOMARU*

The disk of the sun, or *Hinomaru*, in the center of the flag has been an imperial badge since the 14th century. The white field stands for purity and integrity, and some suggest the red disk represents brightness, sincerity, and warmth. The naval ensign is an unusual adaptation of the national flag.

JAPANESE NAVAL ENSIGN

Adopted in 1889, the naval ensign consists of the sun disk with red rays extending to the border of the flag

Rays extend to the edge of the flag to recall the rising sun

AUSTRALIA

Ratio: *2:1*   Adopted: *May 22, 1909*   Usage: *National and Civil*

The Union Jack is retained in the canton

The stars of the Southern Cross

The points of the Commonwealth Star represent the members of the Federation

AUSTRALASIA & OCEANIA

Indonesia   *Papua New Guinea*
AUSTRALIA
New Zealand

THE GREAT SOUTHERN continent of Australia was unified in 1901, as a commonwealth of six formerly separate British subject states.

The first national flag was adopted in 1909 following various design competitions, but its use was restricted. It includes a blue ensign and three motifs, celebrating key aspects of Australian statehood.

THE SOUTHERN CROSS
This constellation is visible throughout the year in southern night skies and has been used as a navigational aid for centuries. It helped guide early European ships to the continent and thus became a popular emblem for the new settlers. The five stars of the cross appear on the fly, with seven points for the brightest stars and five for the lesser *Epsilon Crucis*.

THE UNION JACK
First flown on Australian soil by Captain Cook, it was the national flag from 1788 and remained the official citizens' land flag until 1954. It occupies the canton, denoting Australia's historical links with Great Britain.

THE COMMONWEALTH STAR
This large star affirms the federal nature of government in Australia. Originally there were six points for the six federal states. The seventh · point was added in 1909, to represent the Northern Territory together with the six other external territories administered by the Australian Federal Government.

Australia – State flags

THE STATE FLAGS all use the British Blue Ensign, with the state badge in the canton. The two territories do not follow this pattern.

AUSTRALIAN CAPITAL TERRITORY

The capital territory became self-governing in 1989. The flag, adopted in 1993, depicts Canberra's city coat of arms and the Southern Cross in the city colors of blue and gold.

NEW SOUTH WALES

A gold star adorns each arm of the St. George's Cross, with a golden lion *passant guardant* at the center. This more distinctive badge replaced a previous design in 1876.

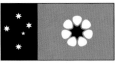

NORTHERN TERRITORY

Adopted by the territory in 1978, the flag depicts the Southern Cross and a stylized Sturt's desert rose against black and ocher, which are the territorial colors.

QUEENSLAND

The state badge depicts the Royal Crown at the center of a Maltese cross. The design of the crown was altered at the coronation of HM Queen Elizabeth II in 1952.

SOUTH AUSTRALIA

The state emblem of the piping shrike (a magpie) is shown with outstretched wings on a yellow background. The piping shrike was adopted as the flag badge in 1904.

TASMANIA

The Red Lion *passant* on a white background recalls historical ties with England and has remained essentially unchanged since its adoption in 1875.

VICTORIA

The Royal Crown was added in 1877. The present arrangement, with the crown surmounting the Southern Cross, became the state arms in 1910.

WESTERN AUSTRALIA

The Black Swan has been Western Australia's emblem since the first British colony was founded at Swan River. The flag was adopted in 1953.

VANUATU

Ratio: *11:18*   Adopted: *February 18, 1980*   Usage: *National and Civil*

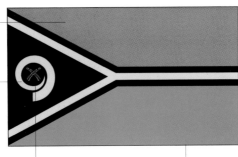

Red is symbolic of blood

The boar's tusk symbolizes prosperity

The yellow Y-shape depicts the outline of the Vanuatu archipelago and the color of sunshine

The fern leaves represent peaceful intentions

Green recalls the richness of the islands

AUSTRALASIA & OCEANIA

VANUATU, FORMERLY KNOWN AS the New Hebrides, was jointly administered by Britain and France from 1906. In 1980, it gained its independence.

During its time as an Anglo-French condominium, the New Hebrides flew the French *Tricolore* side by side with the Union Jack. After the anglophone Vanuaaku Party led the country to independence as Vanuatu in 1980, the colors of the party flag – red, black, green, and yellow – were adopted as the basis for the design of a new national flag. The final design was chosen a few months before independence by a parliamentary committee from designs submitted by a local artist.

THE SYMBOLISM OF THE COLORS
The yellow symbolizes sunshine; the green, the richness of the islands. The red is symbolic of blood, and the

black is for the Melanesian people. The Prime Minister requested the inclusion of the yellow and black fimbriations to give more prominence to the color representing the people. The yellow Y-shape denotes the pattern of the islands in the Pacific Ocean.

THE BOAR'S TUSK
Between the arms of the "Y" lies the traditional emblem of a boar's tusk – the symbol of prosperity worn as a pendant on the islands – crossed by two leaves of the local *namele* fern. The leaves are a token of peace, and their 39 fronds represent the 39 members of Vanuatu's legislative assembly.

FIJI

Ratio: *1:2*   Adopted: *October 10, 1970*   Usage: *National and Civil*

The Union Jack denotes the historical links with Great Britain

The design is based on the British Blue Ensign

The blue field represents the Pacific Ocean

AUSTRALASIA & OCEANIA

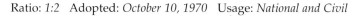

FIJI BECAME PART OF the British Empire in 1784 and an independent nation with dominion status within the Commonwealth in 1970.

The flag was adopted in 1970, when Fiji achieved independence. Its bright blue background symbolizes the Pacific Ocean, which plays an important part in the lives of the islanders, both in terms of the fishing industry, and the burgeoning tourist trade. The Union Jack reflects the country's links with Great Britain.

ARMS OF FIJI
The shield is derived from the country's official coat of arms, which was originally granted by Royal Warrant in 1908. The images depicted on the shield represent agricultural activities on the islands, and the historical associations with Great Britain.

ARMS OF FIJI

The first quarter shows sugar cane, the second a coconut palm, the third a dove of peace, and the fourth a bunch of bananas

On the chief, a British lion holds a coconut between its paws

The coat of arms was granted in 1908. It is a white shield with a red cross and a red chief (the upper third of a shield)

225

PAPUA NEW GUINEA

Ratio: *3:4*   Adopted: *June 24, 1971*   Usage: *National and Civil*

The five stars represent the Southern Cross, and also refer to a local legend about five sisters

A golden bird of paradise

Red and black are the predominant colors in the native art of Papua New Guinea

AUSTRALASIA & OCEANIA

PAPUA NEW GUINEA gained full independence in 1975, following its status as a United Nations Trusteeship under Australian administration.

The Australian administration attempted to introduce Papua New Guinea's first official national flag in 1970. Its choice was a vertically divided flag: blue at the hoist, with the stars of the Southern Cross as in the Australian flag, then white, then green, with a golden bird of paradise. The proposed design was never popular with the local people.

A LOCAL DESIGN

The current flag of yellow and white on black and red was designed by Susan Karike, a local art teacher, and officially accepted in 1971. When Papua New Guinea became independent in 1975, the design was retained as the national flag.

THE COLORS OF NATIVE ART

The colors of the field – red and black – were chosen because of their widespread use in the native art of the country. The bird of paradise has long been a local emblem, and its feathers are used for traditional dress and in festivals and ceremonies.

THE SOUTHERN CROSS

The flag is halved diagonally. The lower half features the Southern Cross constellation in white on black, as it would appear in the night sky over Papua New Guinea. This signifies the link with Australia and also recalls a local legend about five sisters. The red upper half bears a golden bird of paradise in flight.

SOLOMON ISLANDS

Ratio: *5:9* Adopted: *November 18, 1977* Usage: *National and Civil*

The five stars represent the five main groups of islands

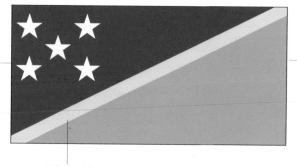

Green represents the land

The yellow stripe symbolizes sunshine

AUSTRALASIA & OCEANIA

THE SOLOMON ISLANDS were a British colony from 1883 until 1976, when they became self-governing, and subsequently independent in 1978.

Before the current flag was adopted in 1977, three different coats of arms had represented the islands.

The national flag, adopted in 1977, is divided diagonally by a stripe of yellow representing the sunshine of the islands. The two triangles formed by the diagonal stripe are blue and green, signifying water and the land. The five stars were initially incorporated to represent the country's five districts. The islands were later divided into seven districts, and the symbolism of the stars was modified to refer to the five main groups of islands.

The coat of arms is also in the colors of the national flag.

ARMS OF THE SOLOMON ISLANDS

The crest is a traditional canoe (in section) and a shining sun

A freshwater crocodile

The national motto – "To lead is to serve"

A shark

The shield depicts frigate birds, an eagle, two turtles, a shield, and bow and arrow, all representing districts of the Solomon Islands

The compartment is a stylized frigate bird

PALAU

Ratio: *5:8*   Adopted: *January 1, 1981*   Usage: *National and Civil*

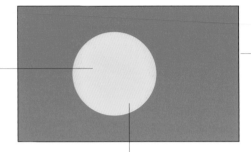

The golden disk depicts the full moon, considered by Palauans to be the best time for celebrations and harvesting

Blue symbolizes the freedom of self-rule

The full moon is set slightly toward the hoist

AUSTRALASIA & OCEANIA

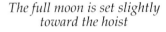

UNDER US CONTROL since 1945, Palau became a republic in 1981. In 1994, it became independent in association with the United States.

The current flag was introduced in 1981 when Palau became a republic. Previously, the flag of the Trust Territory of the Pacific Islands was flown jointly with the United Nations and US flags.

THE SYMBOLISM OF THE FLAG
The flag's very simple design belies the depth of meaning attributed to it. The explanation for the choice of colors is rooted in the history and customs of the Palauan people. The bright blue of the field, which might be assumed to be symbolic of the Pacific Ocean, is in fact a representation of the transition from foreign domination to self-government. The golden disk, which sits slightly off center toward the hoist, represents the full moon. The Palauans consider the full moon to be the optimum time for human activity. At this time of the month, celebrations, harvesting and planting, fishing, tree-felling, and the carving of traditional canoes are carried out. The moon is a symbol of peace, love, and tranquillity.

THE SEAL OF PALAU
Palau does not have a coat of arms, but it has a seal, adopted in 1981, when the country became a republic. The seal is not colored. It depicts a traditional Palauan triangular hut, above the date of adoption. This is surrounded by the title of the state.

MICRONESIA

Ratio: *10:19*   Adopted: *November 30, 1978*   Usage: *National and Civil*

The light blue field recalls the Pacific Ocean

The four stars each represent an island group

The colors are similar to those of the UN flag

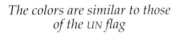

AUSTRALASIA & OCEANIA

Guam   *Marshall Is.*

MICRONESIA

MICRONESIA WAS PART OF the US-administered United Nations Trust Territory of the Pacific Islands, until it became independent in 1979.

The flag, adopted in 1978, is in the colors of the UN flag. The light blue also represents the Pacific Ocean.

In an echo of US practice, the stars represent the four islands, arranged like the points of the compass.

Micronesian States

CHUUK

The white coconut palm shows that the people depend on coconut resources. The white stars represent the 38 municipal units in the territory.

KOSRAE

The olive branches symbolize peace. The four stars signify the islands' four units. The *fafa* stone is traditionally used for grinding food.

POHNPEI

The six stars are for the district's six islands. The half coconut shell represents the *sakau* cup used in traditional ceremonies.

YAP

The outer and inner rings show a *rai*, a traditional symbol of unity. The white outrigger canoe symbolizes the desire to reach the goals of the state.

MARSHALL ISLANDS

Ratio: *10:19*   Adopted: *May 1, 1979*   Usage: *National and Civil*

A 24-pointed star, one for each of the districts on the islands

Blue field for the Pacific Ocean

The two stripes, orange over white, represent the two parallel chains of the Marshall Islands

AUSTRALASIA & OCEANIA

THE MARSHALL ISLANDS were part of the US Trust Territory of the Pacific Islands from 1945 to 1986. They became fully independent in 1990.

The Marshall Islands became a self-governing territory on May 1, 1979, and on that day a new national flag was adopted. Designed by Emlain Kabua, wife of the president of the new government, it was the winning entry in a competition that had attracted 50 designs.

A FLAG FOR A PACIFIC ISLAND

The flag's dark blue field represents the vast area of the Pacific Ocean over which the islands are scattered. The star symbolizes the geographical position of the islands, which lie a few degrees above the Equator. The star has 24 points, representing the 24 municipalities of the Marshall Islands. Four of its rays extend farther than the others and stand for the capital, Majuro, and the administrative districts of Wotji, Yaluit, and Kwajalein. They also form a cross, signifying the Christian faith of the Marshallese.

SYMBOLS OF PROSPERITY

The two parallel stripes extending across the flag symbolize the two parallel chains of the Marshall Islands: the Ratak (Sunrise) Chain is white, the Ralik (Sunset) Chain is orange. The stripes extend and widen upward. This is said to signify the increase in growth and vitality of life on the islands. Orange also symbolizes courage and prosperity, while white represents peace.

NAURU

Ratio: *1:2*   Adopted: *January 31, 1968*   Usage: *National and Civil*

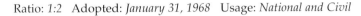

The blue field represents the island's blue skies and the Pacific Ocean

The gold stripe represents the Equator

The 12-pointed star recalls the 12 original tribes of Nauru

AUSTRALASIA
& OCEANIA

Micronesia
NAURU   Kiribati

NAURU WAS JOINTLY ADMINISTERED by Australia, the UK, and New Zealand from 1947 until independence was granted in 1968.

The flag, chosen in a local design competition, was adopted on the day of independence. It depicts Nauru's geographical position, one degree below the Equator. A gold horizontal stripe representing the Equator runs across a blue field for the Pacific Ocean. Nauru itself is symbolized by a white 12-pointed star. Each point represents one of the 12 indigenous tribes on the island.

ARMS OF NAURU
This is also a local design and includes a symbol for the chemical phosphorus; phosphates are Nauru's main export. Beneath it are a frigate bird and a sprig of *tomano*.

ARMS OF NAURU

The symbol for the chemical phosphorus

The shield is surrounded by coconut leaves

A frigate bird

The 12-pointed star, as featured on the flag, representing the 12 tribes of Nauru

The feathers of a frigate bird

A sprig of tomano

KIRIBATI

Ratio: *1:2*   Adopted: *July 12, 1979*   Usage: *National and Civil*

The frigate bird symbolizes command of the sea

The red shield in the coat of arms also depicts a gold flying frigate bird above a rising golden sun

The blue and white wavy bands represent the Pacific Ocean

AUSTRALASIA & OCEANIA

ONCE PART OF the British colony of the Gilbert and Ellice Islands, the Gilberts became independent in 1979 and adopted the name Kiribati.

Kiribati's flag is one of only three national flags that are armorial banners – flags having a design corresponding exactly to that of the shield in the coat of arms.

ARMS OF KIRIBATI

The coat of arms dates back to May 1937 when it was granted to the Gilbert and Ellice Islands, as Kiribati and Tuvalu were then known. The shield was incorporated into the center of the fly half of a British Blue Ensign as the state ensign of the colony.

Shortly before independence was granted in 1979, a local competition was held to choose a new national flag, and a design based on the

colonial coat of arms was submitted to the College of Arms. The College of Arms decided to modify this design. Both the golden frigate bird and the sun were enlarged to occupy more of the top of the flag, and the width of the blue and white wavy bands was reduced.

THE ORIGINAL DESIGN

The local people, however, insisted on the original design, in which the top and bottom halves of the flag were equal, the sun and local frigate bird small, and the various design elements outlined in black.

The new flag was hoisted during the independence day celebrations in the capital, Tarawa, on July 12, 1979.

TUVALU

Ratio: *1:2*   Adopted: *October 1, 1978*   Usage: *National and Civil*

The Union Jack signifies continuing links with Britain

The nine stars are for the nine islands

AUSTRALASIA & OCEANIA

Kiribati

TUVALU

Solomon Is.

THE ELLICE ISLANDS separated from the Gilbert and Ellice Islands in 1975 and adopted the name Tuvalu. Independence was gained in 1978.

Tuvalu means "eight islands" although there are in fact nine, each of which is represented by a star on the flag. The stars' arrangement is supposed to reflect the islands' geographic distribution.

This flag was chosen because it symbolizes the continuing links with Britain and the Commonwealth.

However, anti-Commonwealth feeling rose and in 1995, the government decided on a new flag without the Union Jack. The new flag introduced later that year, retained the stars, but included the arms in a triangle at the hoist. In April 1997 the original design was readopted, following a change of government.

ARMS OF TUVALU

The coat of arms depicts a local meeting house or maneapa

The motto means "Tuvalu for God"

Eight sets of objects reflect the country's title, "Eight Together"

The border contains eight seashells and eight banana leaves

SAMOA

Ratio: *1:2*   Adopted: *January 1, 1962*   Usage: *National and Civil*

The Southern Cross

White represents purity

Red is a traditional Samoan color and symbolizes courage

Blue represents freedom

AUSTRALASIA & OCEANIA

SAMOA
Wallis & Futuna
American Samoa

AT VARIOUS TIMES, Samoa was administered by Germany, the US, and New Zealand. It became the first independent Polynesian nation in 1962.

Prior to 1899, when Samoa was partitioned by Germany and the US, it was ruled by the rival kingdoms of Malietoa and Tamasese.

The flag of Malietoa was probably inspired by missionaries. It was a plain red field, with a white cross and a white star in the canton. The rival King of Tamasese favored the German cause and used flags with black crosses.

A UNITED FLAG
In 1948, and by then a territory of New Zealand, Samoa was granted its current flag. This was created jointly by the kings of Malietoa and Tamasese. It was composed of a red field taken from the former flag of

Malietoa and the Southern Cross from the flag of New Zealand, on a blue field in the canton.

In 1949, the smaller fifth star was added, making the Southern Cross more like that on the Australian flag. The flag was retained when independence was granted in 1962.

ARMS OF SAMOA
The coat of arms was adopted in 1951 and contains symbols reflecting the Christian faith of the Samoan people. It depicts a shield of the Southern Cross, below a coconut palm from the previous colonial badge. Above the shield is a cross recalling the national motto – "May God be the foundation of Samoa."

TONGA

Ratio: *1:2*   Adopted: *November 4, 1875*   Usage: *National and Civil*

The red cross represents the king's devotion to Christianity

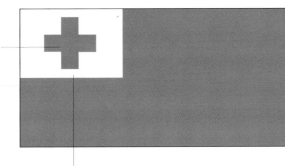

Red represents the blood Jesus shed on the cross

White symbolizes purity

AUSTRALASIA
& OCEANIA

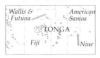

TONGA WAS UNIFIED under King George Tupou I in 1820. In 1900, it became a British protectorate before regaining its independence in 1970.

The flag dates from 1862 when the king at the time, who had converted to Christianity in 1831, called for a national flag that would symbolize the Christian faith.

A NEW "CHRISTIAN" FLAG
The first design was a plain white flag with a red couped cross, but this was later found to be too similar to the International Red Cross flag, adopted in 1863. The white flag was then placed in the canton of a red one. The cross and the red color signify the sacrifice of Christ's blood. The 1875 constitution states that the flag shall never be altered.

The naval ensign, introduced in 1985, also has a red couped cross on white in the canton.

TONGAN NAVAL ENSIGN

Red couped cross in the canton

The naval ensign, introduced in 1985, recalls the flag of Imperial Germany

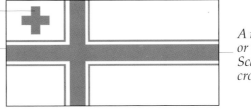

A red, cotised, or bordered, Scandinavian cross

NEW ZEALAND

Ratio: *1:2*   Adopted: *June 12, 1902*   Usage: *National*

The Union
Jack in the
canton
recalls New
Zealand's
colonial ties
to Britain

Four white-
bordered
red stars
represent
the Southern
Cross

*The stars all vary
slightly in size*

AUSTRALASIA
& OCEANIA

NEW ZEALAND WAS SETTLED by the British in the
1800s and was a colony from 1841. It became a
dominion in 1907 and fully independent in 1947.

New Zealand's first flag was
adopted before it became a British
colony. Chosen by an assembly of
Maori chiefs in 1834, the flag was of
a St. George's Cross with another
cross in the canton containing four
stars on a blue field. After the
formation of the colony in 1841,
British ensigns began to be used.

A NEW NATIONAL FLAG
The current flag was designed and
adopted for restricted use in 1869
and became the national flag in
1902. It is the British Blue Ensign,
with a highly stylized representation
of the Southern Cross constellation.
It depicts only four of the five stars
in the constellation.

Overseas Territories

COOK ISLANDS

The 15 stars on the fly represent the
15 main islands of the group; they are
arranged in a ring to indicate that
each island is of equal importance.

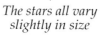

NIUE

The link with the UK is shown by the
use of the Union Jack; that with New
Zealand by the four stars. The large
central star represents Niue itself.

International flags

MANY INTERNATIONAL organizations also adopt flags, below is a selection of the most well-known.

ARAB LEAGUE

ASSOCIATION OF SOUTHEAST ASIAN NATIONS

CARICOM
(Caribbean Community and Common Market)

THE COMMONWEALTH

CIS
(Commonwealth of Independent States)

EUROPEAN UNION

FIAV
(International Federation of Vexillological Associations)

NATO
(North Atlantic Treaty Organization)

OLYMPIC MOVEMENT

ORDER OF ST JOHN

OAU
(Organization of African Unity)

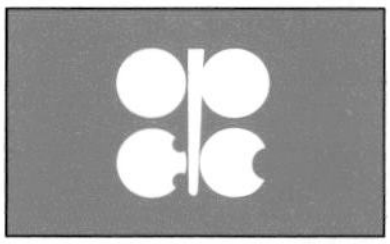

OPEC
(Organization of Petroleum-Exporting Countries)

RED CRESCENT

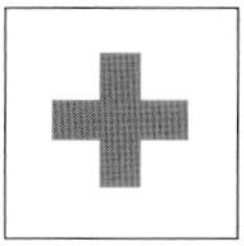

RED CROSS

SOUTH PACIFIC COMMISSION

UNITED NATIONS (UN)

Signal flags

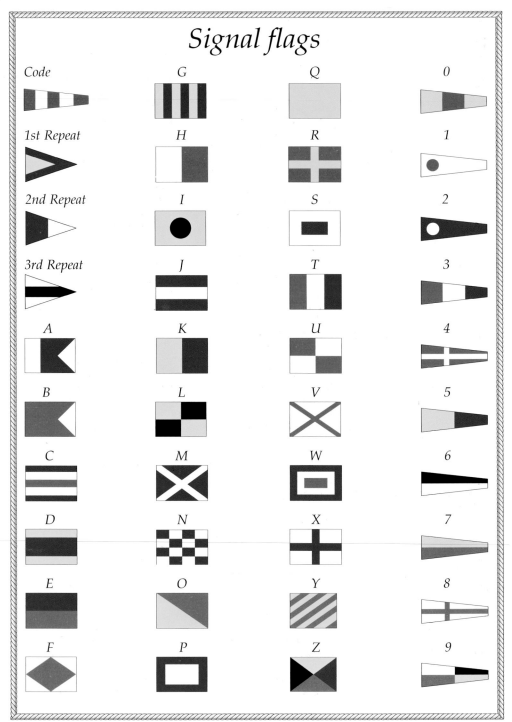

Code	G	Q	0
1st Repeat	H	R	1
2nd Repeat	I	S	2
3rd Repeat	J	T	3
A	K	U	4
B	L	V	5
C	M	W	6
D	N	X	7
E	O	Y	8
F	P	Z	9

INDEX

EUROPE (see front endpaper for World Map)

Svalbard
(to Norway)

Jan Mayen
(to Norway)

ICELAND

Faeroe Is.
(to Denmark)

SWEDEN

FINLAND

NORWAY

ESTONIA

RUSS. FED.

LATVIA

LITHUANIA

RUSSIAN
FEDERATION

UNITED
KINGDOM

DENMARK

REPUBLIC OF
IRELAND

NETH.

POLAND

BELARUS

Isle of Man *(to UK)*

BELGIUM

GERMANY

LUX.

CZECH
REP.

UKRAINE

Channel Islands
(to UK)

FRANCE

SLOVAKIA

SWITZ.

AUSTRIA

HUNGARY

MOLDOVA

LIECH.

SLVNA.

ROMANIA

CROATIA

SAN MARINO

AZERBAIJAN

ANDORRA

MONACO

ITALY

BOS.
&
HERZ.

SERB.
& MON.

BULGARIA

GEORGIA

PORTUGAL

SPAIN

ALBANIA

MACEDONIA

ARMENIA

VATICAN
CITY

GREECE

TURKEY

LEBANON

Gibraltar
(to UK)

MALTA

CYPRUS

SYRIA

I R A N

Madeira
(part of Portugal)

TUNISIA

ISRAEL

IRAQ

Canary Is.
(part of Spain)

MOROCCO

JORDAN

ALGERIA

LIBYA

EGYPT

KUWAIT

WESTERN
SAHARA
(disputed)

SAUDI
ARABIA

MAURITANIA

MALI

NIGER

CHAD

SUDAN

YEMEN

ERITREA